PUBLIC SERVICE UNIONS AND THE EUROPEAN COMMUNITY

To Joanna, Tristan and Stefan

Public Service Unions and the European Community

edited by
EMIL J. KIRCHNER
*Lecturer in Government and
MA Director in Western
European Politics,
University of Essex
and
Research Director,
Association for European
Policy Studies, Brussels*

Gower

Published by

Gower Publishing Company Limited,
Westmead, Farnborough, Hampshire, England.

  British Library Cataloguing in Publication Data

Public service unions and the European Community.
   1. Trade unions—European Economic Community
   countries
   I. Kirchner, Emil J.
   331.88'09 ·   HD6657

   ISBN 0-566-00492-5

Printed and Bound in Great Britain by

Robert Hartnoll Limited, Bodmin, Cornwall.

BSD CS7

Contents

*   This report was based to a large extent on information
    provided in the General Secretariat of the European
    Communities, The Economic and Social Interest Groups
    of Greece (Editions Delta, 1982) pp.103-111.

Tables and Figures

Editor and List of Contributors

Editor

Emil J. Kirchner   University of Essex.
He is author of Trade Unions as a
Pressure Group in the European
Community, and co-author of the
Role of Interest Groups in the
European Community.

Contributors

Bill Beamish   The National Institute for Higher
Education, Limerick.

Jacob Buksti   University of Aarhus.
He is co-author of Danske
Organisationers Lvem Lvad Lvor.

Dan de Vos   Institut d'Etudes Européennes,
Louvain.

Bruno du Ban   European Education and Action
Community, Brussels.

Rob Hartman   Erasmus University.

Nick Hewlett   University of Essex.

Thomas Koeble   University of California,
San Diego.

Jane Sargent   London School of Economics.

Preface

The study of this book has been prepared under the
auspices and financial support of the Association for
European Policy Studies (A.E.P.S.).   A transnational
group of eight researchers assembled the data and reports.
(A listing of the researchers' names can be found at the
end of the book).

The observations are based on information provided by
ten public service unions. Eight comprehensively
structured interviews were conducted with the Secretaries
General and other officials of those unions. In one case
(the German DBB) the same interview scheme was used in
the form of a questionnaire, and for one organisation
(ADEDY of Greece) information supplied by the General
Secretariat of the Economic and Social Committee was used.
The data was collated over a ten month period
(December 1979 to October 1980).

A special word of thanks is to be extended to all the
officials of the unions for the information supplied and
the cooperation provided.

Foreword

As a former Executive Director and current Chairman of
the Research Board of the European Consortium for
Political Research, I take particular pleasure in marking
the occasion of the publication of one of the first
studies of the activities of interest groups of the
countries of the European Community in the European
context. This study is pioneering, in more ways than
one. Thanks to his tireless energy and boundless
enthusiasm, Emil Kirchner has succeeded, in the course
of the last few years, in bringing together and steering
a group of researchers and in collecting and analysing a
large mass of data, not just on the activities of well
known interest groups such as agricultural or industrial
organisations, but of the whole spectrum of bodies which
form the framework of modern democracies. And this
result was achieved with little more than moral support
from the ECPR, which simply did not have the funds to do
more than help the group to meet, develop its research
plans, and coordinate the findings. It is a sad comment
on the state of European social science that it should
be so difficult to find funds to finance the anatomy and
physiology of European interest groups; but there is more
than a ray of light if it is possible to find scholars
who are adventurous enough to undertake and complete the
study in such adverse conditions.

For it is obviously essential that we should know how
interest groups are developing in the member countries
of the EEC and how far this development leads to similar
or to different attitudes towards the European
institutions. Interest groups are the nerves of our
political system, the instruments through which one can
detect demands and discontent, and without which problems
could multiply and, indeed, get out of hand. It is
therefore of major importance to be able to monitor the
extent to which groups representing the various
'living forces' (the forces vives) of the member-nations
of the Ten (soon, probably, Twelve) react to Community
development, how far they endeavour to put pressure at
Community level from within the various countries, and
how far different groups, different branches of economic
and social life become involved in Community life.

Dr. Kirchner and his team have begun this investigation, and they will continue to do so in the coming years, to the greatest benefit of both the public at large, and the politicians, at European and national levels.

I only hope that the publication of this volume will serve to demonstrate to all the importance of the field and to show the value which the continuation of this work has for the scholarly community and for the European public - that is to say, for all of us.

J. Blondel

Colchester, Essex, England.
April, 1981.

Abbreviations

B. EUROPEAN INTEREST ORGANISATIONS

CEM   Council of European Municipalities

CTWUEC   Committee of Transport Workers' Unions in the European Community

ETUC   European Trade Union Confederation

ETUCE   European Trade Union Committee for Education

EULAEE   European Union of Local Authority Employees

EUROFEDOP   European Federation of Employees in Public Services

NFS   Nordic Trade Union Confederation

OEB   European Organisation of Boatmen

USEJF   Union Syndicale Européene des Jeunes Fonctionnaires

C. INTERNATIONAL INTEREST ORGANISATIONS

CIF   International Organisation of National and International Public Service Unions

FIPESO   International Federation of Secondary Teachers

ICFTU   International Confederation of Free Trade Unions

IFFTU   International Federation of Free Teachers

IFTA   International Federation of Teachers' Associations

IFTUTW   International Federation of Trade Unions of Transport Workers

INFEDOP	International Federation of Employees in Public Service
ITF	International Transport Workers' Federation
IULA	International Union of Local Authorities
OECD/TUAC	Organisation for Economic Cooperation and Development/Trade Union Advisory Committee
PSI	Public Service International
PTTI	Postal, Telegraph and Telephone International
TUIPAE	Trade Unions International of Public and Allied Employees
TUITW	Trade Unions International of Transport Port and Fishery Workers
WCL	World Confederation of Labour
WCOTP	World Confederation of Organisations of the Teaching Profession
WFTU	World Federation of Trade Unions
WOTP	World Organisation of the Teaching Profession

D. OTHER ORGANISATIONS

EC	European Communities
ESC	Economic and Social Committee
ILO	International Labour Organisation

1 Introduction
EMIL J. KIRCHNER

Analysis of public service unions has generally centered
on their pressure on governments over wage claims and
working conditions.(1) With a few exceptions (2) less
attention has been given to the perception national
public service unions (3) have on the preparation and
implementation of European Community (EC) policies.

Yet, national civil servants are increasingly affected
by EC legislation, particularly in the agricultural
sector, in employment training schemes, and in value added
tax matters. This raises questions, such as : Do national
public servants perceive the working of the EC as adding
to their workload and/or undermining their authority ?
Feld (1966) argued that national civil servants are, on
the whole, unwilling to relinquish their power of decision
over pressure group demands on the shaping of Community
policy in general, thereby providing additional backing
to the preference of pressure groups for the national
governmental route. He referred to this as the
'gatekeeping' function in the transformation of loyalties
from national interest groups and national bureaucracies
to their European counterparts.(4)

Whilst case studies and surveys are needed to illuminate
the role of national civil servants in the policy making
process of the Community, the emphasis here will be on the
reaction of civil servants to the working of the EC via
their unions. We will identify those areas in which
national public service unions feel affected by the working
of the EC or, conversely, perceive the need to engage in
transnational cooperation and/or lobbying at European
level in order to safeguard and promote their interest.
If lobbying at European level takes place, which channels
(EC Institutions, EC Advisory Committees, or European
Interest Groups) are preferred, with what importance and
intensity ? Another aim will be to learn of the percep-
tions national public service unions have about the role
and effectiveness of their European/International counterparts, especially the International Organisation of
National and International Public Service Unions (CIF).

1

Evidence of this kind will help in assessing whether or not CIF is able to speak for the members or ensure their compliance in the implementation of decisions. Finally, consideration will be given to how national public service unions have adapted administratively to either the working of the EC or CIF, i.e. have there been changes in the staff of secretariats or administrative divisions ? Findings will be related to the Wallace, Wallace, Webb contention that for governmental and non-governmental actors, their activities in the EC are an extension of their regular activities in the domestic arena.(5)

Before dealing with those questions properly, an attempt will be made to look briefly at the national public service sector and their respective unions by identifying structural characteristics, membership strength and links to European/International public service unions. Regarding the latter, emphasis will be given to European public service unions or to the CIF which, though with an international label, consist entirely of European national public service unions. Moreover, only those European/International links are being mentioned which represent, primarily, civil servants, local government authority officials, postal, telegraph and telephone workers, railway employees and teachers. Excluded, therefore, are, for example, the European Metal Federation, which represents both workers from private industry and public workers from nationalised (car manufacturing) industry.

International and European Public Service Unions

With regard to International/European public service unions, a distinction can be made between those which regroup public service unions generally, and those which represent single occupations, such as teachers. General public service unions regroup, primarily, national umbrella public service confederations. The following International/European public service unions are involved :

INTERNATIONAL (General)

The International Organisation of National and International Public Service Unions (CIF)

CIF regroups mainly national independent public service unions of a general kind. Though CIF draws its membership entirely from Europe, indeed nearly exclusively from EC countries, it adopted an international label in order to lobby the ILO and the Council of Europe, as well as the EC.

The Public Services International (PSI) is a so called international trade secretariat of the International Confederation of Free Trade Unions (ICFTU) which comprises unions of a socialist or social democratic orientation. The PSI, like all international trade secretariats, is, however, completely independent of the ICFTU.

The International Federation of Employees in Public Service (INFEDOP) is of a Christian persuasion and acts as a trade secretariat of the World Confederation of Labour (WCL). INFEDOP, in contrast to the PSI, draws its members from a limited number of Western European countries, i.e. those with a Catholic/Christian trade union movement. INFEDOP is affiliated to the WCL, though it is fully autonomous in professional matters. It groups a number of unions in public services, including PTT.

The Trade Unions International of Public and Allied Employees (TUIPAE) belongs to the World Federation of Trade Unions (WFTU), with a Communist ideology, and regroups only a small number of public service unions from Western Europe, mainly, Italy and France.

INTERNATIONAL (Occupational)

The Postal, Telegraph and Telephone International (PTTI) is an international trade secretariat of the ICFTU.

The International Federation of Free Teachers (IFFTU) is an international trade secretariat of the ICFTU.

The World Confederation of Organisations of the Teaching Profession (WCOTP), which claims to be non-governmental and non-political in orientation. The WCOTP was founded in 1952 by the merger of three major international federations of teachers : The World Organisation of the Teaching Profession (WOTP), The International Federation of Teachers' Associations (IFTA) and The International Federation of Secondary Teachers (FIPESO). The IFTA and the FIPESO became constituent federations of the WCOTP.

The World Confederation of Teachers (WCT) is an international professional union of the WCL.

The World Federation of Teachers (WFTU) is an international professional union of the World Federation of Trade Unions.

The International Transport Workers' Federation (IFT) is an international trade secretariat of the ICFTU.

The International Federation of Christian Trade Unions of Railway, Tramway and other Transport Workers (IFTUTW) acts as an international professional union of the WCL.

The Trade Unions International of Transport, Port and Fishery Workers (TUITW) is an international professional union of the WFTU.

EUROPEAN (General)

The European Federation of Employees in Public Services (EUROFEDOP) which regroups the European organisations of INFEDOP (Christian in orientation). EUROFEDOP is an autonomous regional organisation of INFEDOP. The PTT unions are grouped in a PTT Trade Council within EUROFEDOP. EUROFEDOP has 687,000 members (1.1.1979). (For further details see Appendix).

The European Trade Unions Public Service Committee (ETUPSC) functions as an industry committee of the European Trade Union Confederation (ETUC) and was created under the joint efforts of the PSI and EUROFEDOP, from which it draws its member organisations. The ETUPSC represents 4,514,200 members (as of 1.1.1979). A brief description of the ETUPSC and a listing of its member organisations is provided in the Appendix.

The Postal, Telegraph and Telephone International-European Committee (PTTI - European Committee) regroups the European organisations of the PTTI. It consists of the European members of the PTTI Executive Committee and one representative from each country in Europe where the PTTI has affiliates. The affiliated organisations (where there is more than one) in each country decide themselves who shall represent the country. The Committee is also open to observers from affiliated organisations who may take part in the debates of the Committee. For the purposes of the Committee, Turkey is included as European. The 34 organisations of the PTTI - European Committee represent 1,104,320 members (1.1.1981).

The member organisations of the PTTI - European Committee are mentioned in the Appendix.

The European Trade Union Committee for Education (ETUCE) gathers European member organisations of the IFFTU, the WCT and those European members of the WCOTP which belong to a trade union in membership of the ETUC, or which have a working relationship with such a centre. It has 56 organisations and represents 2 million teachers. The ETUCE, thus, represents a great achievement in teacher unity. Further details, especially on membership, are noted in the Appendix.

The Committee of Transport Workers' Unions in the European Community (CTWUEC) operates as an industry committee of the ETUC and was established under the joint efforts of the International Transport Federation (ITF) and the International Federation of Trade Unions of Transport Workers (IFTUTW). (see Appendix).

Having dealt with the respective European/International public service unions, let us now take a look at the public service sector and its trade union structure in the individual EC countries, except for Greece, for which no comparable data was available at the time of writing.

National Public Service Unions

The ten countries are listed in alphabetical order.

1. Belgium

Belgium had 668,000 (1979)(6) public employees, of which 60% represented civil servants, and 40% manual workers. The approximately 622,000 unionised Belgian public employees (93% of the total) are regrouped in the following unions :-

	The Confederation of Christian Trade Unions (CSC)			The Belgian General Federation of Labour (FGTB)			The General Centre of Liberal Trade Unions of Belgium (GSLB)	The Cartel of Independent Trade Unions of Belgium
Total Membership (1980)	1.3 million			1.1 million			165,000	114,000
Membership in public employment(7) (1979)	240,000 (from a wide spectrum of public services)			280,000			50,000 (primarily civil servants)	52,000 (20,000 represent civil servants and 30,000 manual public employees)
Individual Public Employee Unions	Membership Strength	Link at European Level	Individual Public Employee Unions	Membership Strength	Link at European Level		Most public services are regrouped in the Syndicat Libéral des Services Publics	There are 11 member organisations, including :
Centre of Public Services	85,000	EUROFEDOP and ETUPSC	The Centrale Général des Services Publics represents 11 sectors,(8), the largest of which are local authority officials	62,000	ETUPSC			- the Royal Union of Finance Personnel
Railway, Post, Telegraph and Telephone	57,000		Railway	55,000	CTWUEC			- the Postal Federation
FTC (teachers)	50,000		Teachers	50,000	ETUCE			- the General Independent Federation of Personnel in the Ministry of National Defence
Technical Teachers	34,000	ETUCE	Civil Servants in Ministries	39,000	ETUPSC			- the Independent Union of Belgian Railway Workers
Free Teachers	17,000		Post Office workers	30,000	PTTI - European Committee			- the Independent Union of Personnel in Telegraph, Telephone and Marine
UCEO (teachers)	7,000		Telephone and Telegraph	18,000				The Cartel is a member of CIF.
			Public Transport	10,000	CTWUEC			

6

2. Denmark

There were 692,000 (1979) public employees in Denmark, of which approximately 575,000 (83%) were unionised in 1979, mainly through the following unions :-

The Danish Federation of Trade Unions (LO)

Total Membership (1980): 1.1 million

Membership in public employment (1979): 300,000

Individual Public Employee Unions	Membership Strength	Link at European Level
National Union of Commerce and Office Employees	80,000 (in public service)	ETUPSC
DPF (postal)	13,500	PTTI - European Committee
Dansk Funktionaer-forbund (civil servants)	13,400	
COTD (telephone)	7,000	PTTI - European Committee

The Federation of Danish Civil Servants and Salaried Employees Organisation (FTF)

Total Membership (1980): 210,000

Membership in public employment (1979): 150,000

Individual Public Employee Unions	Membership Strength	Link at European Level
Public School Teachers	56,320	ETUCE
Nurses	33,937	ETUPSC
State Civil Servants	27,835	
Nursery School Teachers	16,050	
Municipal Officers in Copenhagen	7,991	ETUPSC
Police	7,008	
Teachers in Special Schools	7,374	
Employees in care of mentally deficient	4,610	
Hospital laboratory workers	4,357	
Social educators	4,138	
Telephone employees	4,015	PTTI - European Committee

The Danish Confederation of Professional Associations (DCPA)

Total Membership (1980): 105,000

Membership in public employment (1979): 40,000

(Direct membership)

One-third of the public employees represented by the DCPA are civil servants.

At European level, teachers are aligned to the ETUCE.

In addition, the **Danish Municipal Workers**, an independent public service union, has 85,000 members and is affiliated, at European level, to the ETUPSC.

A staff of 3,640,000 (1979) make up the French public sector, of which 2,200,000 are civil servants with permanent posts, 650,000 are civil servants with non-permanent posts, and 790,000 are local authority employees.(8) Civil servants are classed into four categories, which in order of importance are A, B, C and D. Public employees belong, mainly, to the following unions :-

	Confédération Générale du Travail (CGT)	Confédération Française Démocratique de Travail (CFDF)	Confédération Générale du Travail - Force Ouvrière (CGT-FO)	Fédération de l'Education Nationale (FEN)	Confédération Générale des Cadres (CGC)	Confédération des Travailleurs Chrétiens (CFTC)
Total Membership (1980)	approx. 2.5 million	1.1 million	800,000	approx. 600,000	300,000	150,000
Membership in public employment (1979)	N.A.	N.A.	approx. 350,000 (2/3rds are lower grade administrators in the civil service and Post Office)	approx. 550,000 represents the majority of teachers in France	approx. 50,000	N.A.

Individual Public Employee Unions / Membership Strength / Link at European Level

Confederation	Individual Public Employee Unions	Membership Strength	Link at European Level
C.G.T.	Cheminots	N.A.	CTWUEC
CFDF	Fédération Démocratique des Travailleurs des PTT (CFDF)	30,000	EURO-FEDOP and ETUPSC
	Syndicat National Unifié des Douanes CFDT	6,000	
	Fédération des Personnels des Communes et OPHLM	8,000	
	Fédération CFDT de la Police Nationale	1,500	
	F.G.T.E./CFDT		CTWUEC
CGT-FO	Fédération des Personnels des Services Publics et des Services de Santé, FO	90,000	ETUPSC
	Fédération Generale des Fonctionnaires, FO	47,500	
	Fédération Nationale des Syndicats des Industries de l'Energie Electrique et du Gaz, FO	18,000	
	Fédération Nationale de l'Education et de la Culture, FO		ETUCE
	Fédération FO Cheminots	22,500	CTWUEC
	Fédération FO Transports	6,000	
	Fédération Syndicaliste des Travailleurs des P.T.T. (FO)	55,000	PTTI - European Committee
FEN			ETUCE
CGC	Fédération Française des cadres de la Fonction Publique (FFCFP), (It represents top civil servants of the A & B categories).	20,000	CIF

N.A. = Not Available.

In addition, there are some specialised independent public service unions, such as the Fédération Autonome des Syndicats de Police (80,000 members)

8

4. Germany

Germany has approximately 3,753,000 (1979) public employees, of which approximately 2,000,000 are in the civil service; half of those, again, can be seen as civil servants (Beamte). One-third are salaried employees (Angestellte), and nearly one-fourth wage-earners (Arbeiter).(9) The civil servants differ from the others not only in their right, their duties, and their terms of employment, but also in the procedures by which these are determined.(10) The principle of an industry-based union structure, otherwise typical for the German system, does not extend to the public sector. Approximately 3.3 million (1979) of the German public employees (88% of the total) belong to the following unions :-

	German Federation of Trade Unions (DGB)		German Federation of Civil Servants (DBB)		German Salaried Staff Union (DAG)	Christian Trade Union Federation of Germany	
	Membership Strength	Link at European Level	Membership Strength	Link at European Level		Membership Strength	Link at European Level
Total Membership	7.9 million (1980)		825,000 (1979)		485,000 (1980)	200,000 (1980)	
Membership in public employment	2.0 million (1979)		825,000 (1979) The DBB comprises the majority of unionised civil servants in Germany.		120,000 approx. (1979)	30,000 approx. (1979)	
Individual Public Employee Unions (the most important only)	Share of public servants:				The DAG is a direct membership organisation and the 120,000 public employees are entirely salaried personnel.		
Union for Public Service, Transport and Communication (ÖTV) (primarily salaried public employees and wage earners)	approx. 710,000	ETUPSC	Railway Officials (GDPA) 105,000			Public Service (GÖD) 8,000	EUROFEDOP and ETUPSC
Postal Union	450,000	PTTI – European Committee	Union of Education (VBE) 100,000	ETUCE		Postal Union 8,000	
Railway Workers Union (Gded)	406,600	CTWUEC	Tax Officials (DSTG) 72,000				
Police Union	166,000		Local Government Officials (Komba) 71,000				
Union of Education and Science (GEW)	125,745	ETUCE	Postal Union 50,000	EUROFEDOP & ETUPSC			
Teachers Union (DLV)	120,500		The DBB is a member of the CIF				

In addition, there are a number of specialised independent unions like : The German Federation of Armed Forces (DBWV) with 250,000 members, The German Federation of Judges (DRB) with 13,000 members, and The Federation of German Border Police (BGV) with 10,000 members. The DBB and DGB compete for their civil service membership, and differ in some of their objectives. As pointed out by Kellner,

" Though their pay demands are generally on the same level quantitatively, their differences on the reform of the legal regulation of conditions of service are unlikely to yield to compromise. A considerable polarisation of opinion was evident in a controversy in the early 1970's over the reform of the law on personnel representation (Personal Vertretungsgesetz). The two confederations differ further in that the DBB has aims over and above those of a trade union : to defend the status interests of civil servants." (11)

Consisting primarily of civil servants, the DBB places considerably more emphasis on the special status of the civil servants than the unions of the DGB. To maintain certain privileges associated with the special status, like job tenure and higher pension prospects, the DBB, in contrast to the DGB unions, prefers that civil servants are treated under public rather than private law (employer-employee relationship) and is opposed to attempts to legalise the right of strike for them.(12)

5. Ireland

Ireland had approximately 220,000 (1979) public employees. The majority of Irish unions are members of the Irish Trade Union Congress (ITUC) to which most of the public employee unions are affiliated.

	Total Membership (1980)	Membership in public employment (1980)	Link at European Level
ITUC	500,000	160,000 approx.	
Individual unions of the ITUC :			
Association of Secondary Teachers	5,000	5,000	
Irish Transport & General Workers Union (ITGWU)	150,000	N.A.	
Association of Scientific, Technical & Managerial Staff (ASTMS)	20,200	N.A.	
Local Government & Public Services Union (LGPSU)	16,000	16,000	EUROFEDOP and ETUPSC
Civil Services Staff Association	12,000	12,000	EUROFEDOP and ETUPSC
Institute of Professional Civil Servants	5,000	5,000	EUROFEDOP and ETUPSC

	Total Membership (1980)	Membership in public employment (1980)	Link at European Level
ESB Officers Association	4,000	4,000	EUROFEDOP and ETUPSC
Civil Service Executive Union	4,000	4,000	ETUPSC
Association of Officers of Taxes	1,500	1,500	ETUPSC
Post Office Workers' Union	10,500	10,500	PTTI – Euro. Committee
Irish Post Office Engineering Union	7,000	7,000	PTTI – Euro. Committee
Post Office Management Staffs' Association	1,000	1,000	PTTI – Euro. Committee
Irish Municipal Employees' Trade Union	2,000	2,000	
Civil Service Alliance	1,700	1,700	
Irish National Teachers' Organisation	22,000	22,000	
Teachers Union of Ireland	5,000	5,000	

N.A. = Not Available.

The Italian public sector comprises a staff of 3,126,000 (1979). Public employees are mainly represented in the following unions :-

	Italian Confederation of Labour (CGIL)		Italian Confederation of Labour Unions (CISL)		Italian Labour Union (UIL)		Italian Confederation of Independent Labour Unions (CISAL)		Italian Confederation of National Labour Unions (CISNAL)	DIRSTAT Federazione fra le Associazioni e i Sindicati Nazionale dei Quadri Direttivi della Funzione Publica
Total Membership (1980)	approx. 3,5 million		approx. 2,5 million		approx. 1,5 million		300,000		80,000	11,000
Membership in public employment (1979)	approx. 1,1 million		approx. 600,000		approx. 300,000		approx. 80,000		approx. 50,000	11,000
Individual Public Employee Unions (some of these unions)	Member-ship Strength	Link at European Level	Member-ship Strength	Link at European Level	Member-ship Strength	Link at European Level	Member-ship Strength	Link at European Level	CISNAL draws most of its public service members from the central administration (ministries).	The 33 affiliated federations of DIRSTAT represent approximately 40,000 higher civil servants in Italy (the rest is not affiliated to any union). DIRSTAT was affiliated to CIF until 1979.
Hospital workers	90,000		Elementary School Teachers 100,000	ETUCE	State Officials 116,000		Electricity 18,000	ETUPSC		
Bus, Tram and Railway workers	75,000	CTWUEC	Local Government Officials 90,000		Local Government Officials 81,200					
State Officials	44,000		State Officials 60,605		Public Employees 30,000					
PTT	35,000	PTTI - Euro. Comm.	Transport 50,000	CTWUEC	Transport 20,000	CTWUEC				
Telecommunications	12,000		Electricity 43,857		PTT 13,000	PTTI - Euro. Comm.				
Gas	8,000		Employees of State supervised and State enrolled agencies 43,800							
Electricity	5,000		PTT 35,000	PTTI - Euro. Comm.						
			Telecommunications 11,000							
			Local Agencies of P.T. 40,000							

In addition, there are a number of specialised independent public employee unions, such as :-
- the National Independent Grammar Schools Union (25,000 members)
- the National Association of Judges (4,700 members)
- the Union of Italian Judges

7. Luxembourg

Luxembourg had 18,300 (1979) public employees. The approximately 17,000 (1979) unionised public employees (93% of the total) are represented in the following unions :-

	Confédération Générale du Travail de Luxembourg (CCT-Lux)	Confédération des Syndicats Chrétiens (LCG)	Confédération Générale de la Fonction Publique (CGFP)
Total Membership (1980)	35,000	15,000	12,700
Membership in public employment (1979)	approx. 1,900	approx. 2,400	12,700

CCT-Lux:

Individual Public Employee Unions	Membership Strength	Link at European Level
FNCTTFEL	1,500 (public service sector only)	- CTWUEC - PTTI - European Committee - ETUPSC

LCG:

Individual Public Employee Unions	Membership Strength	Link at European Level
Employees and civil servants FCEF		
Public Service workers (FCPSP)	1,000	EUROFEDOP and
Transport (FCPT)	1,400	ETUPSC

CGFP:

The CGFP is a direct membership union and represents the bulk of civil servants and a substantial part of public employees in Luxembourg. It draws its members from every public sector.

The CGFP is affiliated to the CIF

8. The Netherlands

There are 694,000 (1979) public servants in Holland. The approximately 585,000 (1979) unionised public servants (89% of the total) are represented in the following way :-

	Federation of Dutch Trade Unions (FNV)			The Christian National Federation (CNV)			Ambtenarencentrum
Total Membership (1980)	1.1 million			300,000			105,700
Membership in public employment (1979)	310,000			170,000			105,700
Individual Public Employees Unions	Membership Strength	Link at European Level		Individual Public Employees Unions	Membership Strength	Link at European Level	The biggest affiliated unions are :-
General Union of Public Servants and Health, Welfare and Employment Services' Personnel (ABVA/KABO)	250,000	ETUPSC PTTI - Euro. Comm.		Civil Servants and Public Health (NCBO)	62,000	EUROFEDOP and ETUPSC	a. State Personnel (25,289) b. Teachers (16,629) c. Seamen (14,420) d. Communal Officials (13,520)
Teachers' Union (ABOP)	40,000	ETUCE		Public Officials (ARKA)	33,500		e. Royal Non-Commissioned Officers Association (8,253)
Police Union (NPB)	17,000			Teachers (PCO)	29,000	ETUCE	f. The National Corporals Association (5,640)
				State and Municipal Police (ACP)	19,500		The Ambtenarencentrum is a member of CIF and the Teachers' Union GNL is affiliated to the ETUCE.

14

9. The United Kingdom

There are approximately 4,400,000 (1979) public employees in Great Britain, of which 750,000 are in the civil service, 1,000,000 in the national health service, and 3,000,000 in local authorities.(13) Basically, two categories of public employees can be distinguished.(14) These are :-

1. Central or local government employees, known as the civil service. Employees may be manual or industrial workers (found in various maintenance, construction or manual manufacturing jobs in government establishments), or non-industrial civil servants (engaged in executive and administrative duties for government ministries).

2. Local authorities of local government services engaged in a wide range of activities delegated by central government, including education, police, fire, protection and local transport.

Most British unions are members of the Trade Union Congress (TUC), which also represents 3.5 million (80% of the total) public servants (1979).

	Total Membership	Membership in public employment	Link of Public Employees Unions at European Level
Trade Union Congress (TUC)	11 million (1979)	3.5 million (1979)	

Individual unions of the TUC :-

Public Employees

National and Local Government Officers Association (NALGO)	753,226	CIF
National Union of Public Employees (NUPE)	712,392	ETUPSC
National Union of Teachers	291,239	WCOTP and ETUCE

	Total Member-ship	Membership in public employment	Link of Public Employees Unions at European Level
Confederation of Health Service Employees		215,033	ETUPSC
National Association of Schoolmasters and Union of Women Teachers		111,566	WCOTP and ETUCE
National Association of Teachers in Further and Higher Education		65,269	WCOTP and ETUCE
Educational Institute of Scotland		46,985	WCOTP and ETUCE
Association of University Teachers		29,248	
Fire Brigades Union		30,000	ETUPSC
Greater London Council Staff Association		17,225	
Health Visitors Association		10,881	

Civil Servants and Post Office

Civil and Public Service Association		224,780	ETUPSC and PTTI - Euro. Committee
Union of Post Office Workers		197,157	PTTI - Euro. Committee
Post Office Engineering Union		121,406	PTTI - Euro. Committee
Society of Civil and Public Servants		106,903	
Institute of Professional Civil Servants		99,051	ETUPSC
Inland Revenue Staff Federation		67,614	ETUPSC

16

	Total Member- ship	Membership in public employment	Link of Public Employees Union at European Level
Civil Service Union		46,928	ETUPSC
Society of Post Office Executives		22,567	PTTI - Euro. Committee
Prison Officers Association		22,189	
Association of Post Office Management Staff		18,500	PTTI - Euro. Committee
Association of Government Supervisors and Radio Officers		12,138	
Association of First Division Civil Servants		8,149	

Railways

	Total Member- ship	Membership in public employment	Link of Public Employees Union at European Level
National Union of Railwaymen	178,000	180,000	
Transport Salaried Staffs' Association	67,000	69,479	CTWUEC
Locomotive Engineers and Firemen, Associated Society	27,000	27,738	

Other Unions with Public Employees

	Total Member- ship	Membership in public employment	Link of Public Employees Union at European Level
Transport and General Workers' Union	2,072,818	40,000	ETUPSC and CTWUEC
Electrical, Electronic and Telecommunications Union - Plumbing Trade Union	420,000	20,000	ETUPSC

	Total Member- ship	Membership in public employment	Link of Public Employees Unions at European Level
Association of Scientific, Technical and Managerial Staff	471,000	10,000	ETUPSC and CTWUEC

There are three types of trade union in Britain. Craft, or occupational unions, that represent workers with a specific craft, irrespective of the industry in which they are employed; industrial unions, which organise workers in a single industry, irrespective of their craft, occupation or grade of skill; and general unions, which organise on the basis of the principle of being 'one big union'. These are prepared, in theory, to admit any worker but, in practice, fill the gap in trade union organisation left by the craft and industrial unions. Their main strength is, thus, among labourers and semi-skilled workers.

NALGO, the largest of the public employee/service unions within the TUC,is a hybrid of the craft and industrial unions representing, as it does, white collar workers from any public service industry. As NALGO extends its membership from purely local government into the nationalised industries, it is developing more the characteristics of a general union. As such, it competes for members in the public services with unions organised on the basis of each of the three types mentioned above.

Cross Country Comparison of the Public Service Sector

As can be seen from Table 1.1, the EC countries, except Greece, compose 17 million public employees; around 20 per cent of the labour force in the Community. The degree of unionisation of public employees in the EC countries is in the 80 to 90 per cent range, which is considerably higher than for the private sector.(15) Moreover, with membership of blue collar unions generally declining, whilst that of public service unions is rising (16), the pattern of industrial relations might change. This might also affect the party political allegiance held by umbrella trade union confederations, such as the TUC, to which public service unions are affiliated.

TABLE 1.1

Extent of Public Service Employment and Degree of Unionisation (1979)

	Belgium	Denmark	France	Germany	Ireland	Italy	Luxem-bourg	Nether-lands	United Kingdom	TOTAL
Members of civilian employees (in 1,000)	3,128	2,096	17,491	21,476	834	14,521	135	4,314	22,920	87,176
Public service employees (in 1,000)	668	692	3,640	3,753	220	3,126	18,3	694	4,400	17,209
% of civilian employment	21.35	33.01	20.81	17.47	26.37	21.53	12.22	16.08	19.20	19.74
Unionised public service employees (in 1,000)	620	575	N.A.	3,300	N.A.	N.A.	17	585	3,550	
% of unionised public service employees	92.81	83.09	N.A.	87.93	N.A.	N.A.	92.90	84.29	80.68	

Source : EUROSTAT : EUROSTATISTICS : Data for short term economic analysis, no.7-8, 1982, Statistical Office of the European Communities, Luxembourg, p.25, and EUROSTAT : National Accounts ESA - detailed tables by branch 1970-79, Statistical Office of the European Communities, Luxembourg, 1981.

Research Aims and Criteria

In the following, an attempt is made to analyse the linkage between the activities of public service unions at the national and European level. It provides systematic information on how national public service unions in the EC countries were structured in 1980, and in what form they sought to influence legislation at national and European level. The organisational features of these national public service unions, such as functions and decision-making styles of administrative bodies, or relationship with affiliates, will be treated together with their aims and policy priorities. Further coverage of these unions concerns their treatment of Community affairs, their relations with their European/ International counterparts (primarily CIF), and their level of transnational cooperation.

National public service unions were selected, which were either affiliated to the International Organisation of National and International Public Service Unions (CIF), or comprised, primarily, personnel of the central (or federal) government, provinces (or lander) and local authorities, or of such public sectors as the railway, post office and education. To a lesser extent, there will be a concern for employees of public or quasi public corporations, although a distinction cannot always clearly be made since some of the unions treated in this study, like the Belgian Cartel, recruit members from both.

Some of the main reasons for selecting CIF and its member organisations for this study were :-

(a) Since, with one exception, all its affiliates come from EC countries, its member organisations appeared as primary candidates for an examination of EC implementation and involvement; and

(b) CIF affiliates pledge not to have any formal links to political parties, and are thus free of party political ideologies on pro or anti EC stands.

The following is a brief description of CIF's structure and aims :

20

The International Organisation of National and International Public Service Unions (CIF)

Founded in 1955 as an organisation representing senior officials, CICF, as it was then known, changed its designation following the accession of organisations such as NALGO (1961) covering many grades of officers. Its highest decision-making body is the Congress (meeting tri-annually) followed by the Governing Council (meets twice a year), and the Executive Board (meets two to three times a year). The Secretariat is managed and founded on a rotating basis by one of the member organisations for a period of three years.

According to Article 6.1 of the Statute, membership of CIF is open to : "(a) trade unions of public servants or similar occupational organisations in individual countries; (b) national groupings of such bodies; (c) international organisations of particular categories of public servants; and (d) organisations of the staff of intergovernmental, international and supranational bodies." The constitution of CIF forbids activities with a party political or ideological connection, and membership is restricted to organisations of a non-political nature, although this does not, necessarily, imply that it does not take political action.

CIF's aims and priorities are to promote the interests of public servants before international, intergovernmental and supranational organisations, especially the European Community and the International Labour Organisation. More specifically, this entails :-

1. Harmonisation of the national laws covering public servants and employees.

2. The maintenance and furtherance of adequate remuneration and working conditions for civil servants and public employees.

3. The maintenance and strengthening of an independent trade union movement for the public service, both nationally and internationally.

CIF represents close to 2 million civil servants/public employees. The majority of affiliates are civil servants, although a third are local government officers. CIF membership is, with one exception, (a Swiss organisation) based on EC countries.

CIF has the following member organisations :-

Country	Name of Organisation	Membership Strength	
Belgium	Cartel des Syndicats Indépendants de Belgique	52,000	(1979)
France	Fédération Française des Cadres de la Fonction Publique (FFCFP)	20,000	(1979)
Germany	Deutscher Beamtenbund (DBB)	825,000	(1979)
Luxembourg	Confédération Générale de la Fonction Publique (CGFP)	12,700	(1979)
Netherlands	Ambtenarencentrum	105,000	(1979)
Switzerland	Vereinigung der Höheren Bundesbeamten (VHB)	3,500	(1979)
United Kingdom	National and Local Government Officers (NALGO)	782,343	(1980)
	Total	1,800,543	

International affiliations : Federation of European Railway Officials

Federation of European Postal Officers

Notes

(1) Concerns have been expressed, for example, that
    their increasing pressure diminishes democracy. See
    Sanford Cohen, 'Does Public Employee Unionism
    Diminish Democracy?'. Industrial and Labour Review,
    vol.32, no.2, January 1979, p.189.

(2) Notable exceptions are : Helen Wallace, 'The Impact
    of Communities on National Policy Making',
    Government and Opposition, vol.6, 1971, pp.528-538;
    William Averyt, 'Eurogroups, Clientela, and the
    European Community', International Organisation,
    vol.29, no.4, Autumn 1975, pp.949-972; Werner Feld,
    'Implementation of the European Community's Common
    Agricultural Policy : expectations, fears, failures',
    International Organisation, vol.33, no.3, Summer 1979,
    pp.335-363; and Jane Sargent, 'The British Banker's
    Association and the EC', Journal of Common Market
    Studies, vol.XX, no.3, March 1982, pp.269-286.

(3) Not all scholars agree on the term 'union', preferring
    instead the definition of 'association'. Central to
    this distinction is the latter's standing on strike
    or, conversely, privileges derived from national
    labour legislation. For example, the German
    Federation of Civil Servants (DBB), rigorously
    opposes transferring their relationship from one of
    public to private law, insisting instead on the
    special relationship of the civil servant to his
    government, rather than as an employer-employee
    relationship. The DBB not only opposes use of the
    strike by civil servants, but would also oppose
    any attempts to legalise the strike for them.
    For further details, see William H. McPherson,
    Public Employee Relations in West Germany, The
    University of Michigan-Wayne State University,
    Ann Arbor, 1971. See also Klaus von Beyme,
    Challenge to Power : trade unions and industrial
    relations in capitalist countries, (Sage Publications
    Ltd., 1980), especially Chapter I.

(4) Werner Feld, 'National Economic Interest Groups and
    Policy Formation in the EEC', Political Science
    Quarterly, vol. LXXXI, no.2, June, 1966, p.407.

(5) Helen Wallace, William Wallace and Carole Webb (eds.),
    Policy Making in the European Communities
    (John Wiley & Sons, 1977), Chapter 12.

(6) Figures on public employment for all EC countries
    have been taken from EUROSTAT for 1979. See
    EUROSTAT : National Accounts ESA - Detailed tables
    by branch 1970-79, Statistical Office of the
    European Communities, Luxembourg, 1981.

(7) Public employment figures of the CSC, FGTB and
    CGSLB are based on : (a) trend statistics provided
    by Armand Spineux, 'Forces et Politiques Syndicales
    en Belgique', Dissertation doctorale en Sociologie,
    1981; and (b) material provided by the CSC.

(8) See F.F. Ridley (ed.), Government and Administration
    in Western Europe (Martin Robertson, 1979), p.90.

(9) Berndt K. Keller, 'Public Sector Labour Relations in
    West Germany', Industrial Relations, vol.17, no.1,
    February 1978, p.19.

(10) For an excellent description and analysis see
     William H. McPherson, op. cit., p.21.

(11) See Berndt K. Keller, 'Determinants of the Wage Rate
     in the Public Sector : the Case of Civil Servants in
     the Federal Republic of Germany', British Journal
     of Industrial Relations, November 1981, pp.348-349.

(12) See William H. McPherson, op. cit., pp.169-170.

(13) See F.F. Ridley, op. cit., p.22.

(14) See David Winchester, 'Labour Relations in the Public
     Sector in the United Kingdom', Charles M. Rehmus (ed.),
     Public Employment Labour Relations : An Overview of
     Eleven Nations (Ann Arbor : Institute of Labour and
     Industrial Relations, The University of Michigan-
     Wayne State University, 1975), pp.64-66.

(15) Union density in the public employment sector, as
     shown by Clegg for the early 1970's, was between
     35 per cent (United Kingdom) and 50 per cent (France
     and West Germany) higher than for private manual
     employment, and exceeded the percentage in private

white collar employment by 48 percent in the United
Kingdom, 60 per cent in France, and 72 per cent in
West Germany. Hugh Clegg, 'Trade Unionism under
Collective Bargaining : A Theory based on Comparisons
of Six Countries', (Basil Blackwell, 1976), p.12.
See also Klaus von Beyme, op. cit., pp.42-44.

(16) See The Observer (Business Section) of 4.4.1982.

2

Cartel des Syndicats Indépendants de
Belgique (Cartel of Independent
Trade Unions of Belgium

Secretary General : J. Bollaerts

Address : Bd. Bischoffsheim 36
100 Bruxelles.

Tel. (02) 218 73 98

I. ORGANISATIONAL FEATURES

1. Date of Establishment

1926 (although the Postal Federation, its predecessor, had existed since 1908).

2. Membership Size

The Cartel has approximately 52,000 members. Any agent of the state (government employee), parastate at regional or communal level, is eligible for membership of the Cartel, together with members of all public services.

3. Administrative Bodies

(a) The National Sectoral Committees - Each of the eleven branch sectors has a national committee composed of delegates chosen from among the members, in accordance with each sector's rules of procedure. These committees prepare the policy documents for the sectors, which must be approved by the members, organises union activities for the sector, and makes contacts with local sections. They also appoint representatives to the General Council and transmit to the Secretary General of the Cartel minutes of committee meetings, as well as their demands, resolutions, memoranda and agenda.

(b) The Congress determines the general aims of the Cartel's programme of action. The congresses are organised at the demand of the General Council, or of the Directors' Committee.

(c) The General Council is the sovereign authority of the Cartel and is composed of members of the Directors' Committee, and delegates from the National Sectoral Committees, the number of delegates being determined by the 'Règlement d'ordre intérieur'. The General Council has, inter alia, the following functions :-

(1) It specifies the objectives of the Cartel and the means of achieving these, in accordance with the aims fixed by the Congress;

(2) It fixes the annual subscription rates and amends the statutes; and

27

(3) It fixes the number and scope of the
sectors, decides on the acceptance of new
sectors and on their competence to act on the
proposals of the Directors' Committee.

The General Council meets at least twice a year at
the suggestion of the Secretary General, the
Directors' Committee, on the basis of a decision
taken by the General Council, itself, or at the
demand of at least two National Sectoral Committees.

The General Council elects its bureau for one year.
This bureau is composed of a president, a vice-
president, a minutes secretary, and a secretarial
assistant, who acts as a linguist. To be elegible
for election to the bureau, candidates must be
nominated by their own sector, and when a replacement
is required, she/he is chosen by the sector of the
previous member, not by bureau members.

The president oversees the formalisation of the
bureau's powers, and ensures that documents are
transmitted to the relevant bodies. She/he also
chairs the bureau's meetings, informs the police of
their meetings, and calls for votes on particular
issues, when required. The vice-president assists
the president in these duties, and replaces her/him
with full powers whenever the president is indisposed.
The president, vice-president, members of the
Directors' Committee, and both secretaries, have no
voting rights.

(d) The Directors' Committee is constituted by the
Secretary General, the treasurer of the Cartel, and a
delegation from the sectors, with the possibility of
including the assistance of one or more of the
technical experts. Its bureau is the same as that
of the General Council, which also has no voting
rights. The Directors' Committee collectively
manages the Cartel. It prepares the work of the
General Council and takes and executes decisions in
accordance with the directives laid down by the
former.

(e) The Secretary General is elected for a four year
term and is eligible for reelection following a term
of office. The Secretary General makes reports to
the Directors' Committee on the management of the

28

Cartel, with which he is entrusted, and he ratifies
all initiatives of the Directors' Committee.

The Secretary General is authorised to locally
engage the Cartel in all judiciary and civil action,
both nationally and internationally.

(f) Committees - Apart from the committees and the
working and study groups of the Directors' Committee,
the Cartel has no formalised committee structure,
largely because it does not have the finances to
support one.

4. Decision-Making Style

This is always done on the basis of a simple majority vote
of those present in the administrative bodies, given that
there is a quorum. If not, a second vote can be taken,
but not sooner than ten days after the first, where the
vote will be carried, regardless of whether a quorum is
present or not.

Linguistic parity is maintained at all levels of the
organisation.

5. Relationship with Members and Organisational Cohesion

The national structure of the Cartel is, at present,
organised on a professional and a territorial basis, with
sectors corresponding to professions and regions.
Relations between the sectors and the central administration of the Cartel are governed by the 'Règlement
d'Ordre intérieur'. The number and jurisdiction of the
sectors are fixed by the General Council on the basis of
proposals from the Directors' Committee.

Each sector develops its own general rules, the funda-
mental rules having been fixed by the General Council.
The general rules are made within guidelines set by the
Cartel's objectives, which aim to form a union to provide
legal assistance and leisure activities for the members.
The demands of a given sector have no jurisdiction over
other sectors, and are established and defended by the
Sectoral Committees in the name of the Cartel.

The demands which are liable to have an effect on other
sectors are transmitted to the Directors' Committee in the
form of recommendations. As a function of their specific

structure, National Sectoral Committees can create
regional committees in accordance with the rules pertaining.
There are divergences of opinion on particular points of
an issue between different professional and regional
sectors (indemnity allowance differences, etc.), but there
are no fundamental points of disagreement on a par with
the Cartel itself.

6. Personnel of Secretariat and Categories

The Secretariat of the Cartel is composed of :-

> 1 Secretary General
>
> 1 full-time secretary
>
> 2 part-time secretaries
>
> (1 member of the Postal Federation).

7. Budget Size and Contribution Criteria

No details were given of the size of the current budget,
although these could be calculated, as they are based
solely on subscriptions, which average out at 200 BF per
month.

II. AIMS AND PRIORITIES

1. Aims and Objectives

The Cartel holds the following aims and objectives :-

(1) cooperation on the national viewpoint;

(2) coordination of the national view point; and

(3) acting as an important interlocutor with government.

The Cartel aims to promote and defend its members'
interests, and is acting without any political, philoso-
phical commitment or dependence.

2. Policy Priorities

Migrant workers, protection of the environment and energy
policy were regarded as most important, industrial affairs
next most important, with foreign affairs, external trade,
research, science and education, and employment and
vocational training of lesser importance. All other

issues are dealt with as they arise. All contacts regarding these issues take the form of written and oral questions, and rely on personal contacts (for both the European and national levels).

Action programmes are published, but not annually, again due to financial restrictions. Since 1975, annual reports have been drafted, but they have not been published or distributed; instead, they are circulated among a select number of members of the Cartel, the government, and the International Organisation of National and International Public Service Unions (CIF).

III. CHANNELS OF INFLUENCE (National and EC Level)

Essentially, the national level predominates on specific issues because the Cartel, itself, has no specific EC representation, except through CIF and the European Organisation of Boatmen (OEB). The Cartel would, however, like to have direct representation at the Community level.

1. National Level

The Cartel has contacts with government administration, government ministries, parliamentary committees, MPs, and political parties, in that order of importance. Frequency of contacts with these channels is in the same order. The Cartel also has regular contacts with other interest groups. With each of the contacts mentioned, demands are expressed through personal associations, written and oral questions.

2. European Level

In general, CIF and OEB are the two channels through which the Cartel seeks to influence Community institutions, having no direct representation of its own.

IV. TREATMENT OF COMMUNITY AFFAIRS

(see Section V below)

V. RELATIONS WITH EUROPEAN INTEREST GROUPS

1. Relations with CIF

CIF is regarded as the 'international' arm of the Cartel, which thus conducts all the Cartel's relations with the EC.

31

There has been no difference of opinion between CIF and the Cartel on policy issues, and no coordination between the activities of the two since 1972, as the Cartel leaves Community level action entirely up to the CIF.

2. Relations with the OEB

The European Organisation of Boatmen was established in 1976 to liaise with D-G VII (Transport) over the issue of inland waterway navigation, particularly that regarding the Rhine. The OEB has a president, four vice-presidents, and represents four EC countries concerned by this issue. Its members meet at least once a month, and it is recognised by the Commission as a lobbying group.

The OEB operates in conjunction with UNIF (L'Union International de Navigation Fluvial).

Thus, on all issues pertaining to inland waterway traffic, the transport sector of the Cartel operates on Community issues through the OEB, whereas, on all other issues, the Cartel operates through CIF. There is, thus, no liaison between OEB and CIF and they are not regarded as substitute groups.

Sources   Statutes of the Cartel (no date).

Interview   Mr. J. Bollaerts,
             Secretary General of the Cartel

             carried out by,
             Mr. Dan de Vos, March 1980.

3

FTF, Funktionaerernes Og Tjenestemaendenes
Faellesrad (Federation of Danish Civil
Servants' and Salaried Employees'
Organisations)

President : Kirsten Stallknecht

Chief of
Secretariat : Svend Skovbra Larsen

Address : Vesterport, Trommesalen 2,3.
DK-1614 København V.

Tel. (01) 15 30 22

I. ORGANISATIONAL FEATURES

1. Date of Establishment

January, 1952.

2. Membership Size

317,500 (1980). Trend : rising.

3. Administrative Bodies

(a) The Congress is the highest decision-making body
of the FTF. It consists of the Executive Committee
and delegates from all affiliated organisations
elected according to the principles of proportional
representation. In 1978 the Congress consisted of
287 delegates, including the Executive Committee.
The Congress meets every two years.

(b) The Meeting of Representatives is the highest
authority when Congress is not in session. It
consists of the Executive Committee and 30 members
elected by the Sections, once again by proportional
representation. Every Section is allowed to elect a
minimum of two members, which means that the total
number of representatives may exceed 30. In 1978
the Meeting of Representatives included 40 members,
9 of which were from the Executive Committee; it
meets twice a year.

(c) The Executive Committee consists of the President
of the FTF and 8 members elected by Congress. The
Executive Committee determines the general political
strategy and guidelines of the organisation. It
determines activities of the FTF concerning specific
problem areas, normally on the basis of papers
prepared by the Secretariat. The Executive Committee
employs permanent staff and appoints representatives
to public committees, etc.

(d) The FTF-Sections - The affiliated organisations
are grouped into three Sections : Section S (State),
Section K (local and regional authorities), and
Section P (private firms, etc.). The Sections
cannot make decisions binding on FTF. They serve as
contact bodies for the organisation and provide an
arena for discussion on matters that concern the

34

Sections. Finally, they appoint members to the
Meeting of Representatives and, thereby, indirectly,
to the Executive Committee. They meet whenever it is
deemed necessary, but at least once between meetings
of the Congress.

(e) President Meetings - For the purpose of
discussing matters of prime importance, the Executive
Committee may call for a meeting of all presidents
of the affiliated organisations.

(f) Permanent Committees - FTF has established a
number of Permanent Committees : Labour Market and
Manpower Policy, Working Conditions, Education,
Technology and Educational Policy. These committees
were established by the Congress. They are not working
groups, but permanent, and discuss important matters
within their field whenever they arise. They do not
work out programmes, but provide basic material for
the Executive Committee. Decisions are taken by the
Executive Committee.

4. Decision-Making Style

Formal decisions of the FTF can be taken by simple majority,
but in reality unanimity is being practised.

5. Relationship with Members and Organisational Cohesion

As a federation, the FTF does not have individual members.
They are represented by their respective organisations,
who cooperate with the FTF. The FTF is, basically, a
service body and spokesman for the common interests of the
member associations. It seems to have little competence in
relation to the activities of the affiliated organisations
and, basically, serves the purpose of strengthening the
position of white collar workers in relation (a) to blue
collar unions; (b) to employers, whether public or
private; and (c) to narrow the gap between white and blue
collar workers.

Organisational cohesion is, supposedly, ensured by the
representation of all organisations in the Meeting of
Representatives and the Congress. The most general problem
within the FTF arises from the difference of interests
between the public service unions (comprising 75 per cent
of the total) and the private sector. Until the beginning
of the 70's, the conflict between the two sectors was

35

quite severe and culminated, after the agreements with the LO, in a number of small privately employed groups withdrawing from the FTF. The agreement with the LO did, however, indicate that the interests of the public employee workers were of greater importance to the FTF than those of the private sector.

These difficulties still persist today, as the interests of the public employees seem to dominate FTF functions, especially following cuts in public spending. However, the FTF does attempt to secure the interests of privately employed workers, if only to secure unity.

Another source of conflict has been the political diversity of views within the FTF. In the beginning, the political neutrality of the FTF covered a bias towards the bourgeois parties, but the developments of the mid 60's have created a common interest and point of view between important FTF groups and the Social Democratic Party.

Finally, there has been an emerging radical and leftist wing within many FTF organisations - some are even dominated by leftist forces. The maintenance of political neutrality is, therefore, necessary to maintain unity. All of the member associations have to be politically neutral, i.e. not linked to any specific political party, and have the right to conduct their own negotiations on pay and working conditions. They are also free to formulate political statements and entertain contacts to political parties.

Because of the structure of the organisation, and because of the diversity of interests between affiliated organisations, the common principle for decision-making in the FTF is by unanimity. If unanimity is not achieved, the FTF will, normally, not express any views, and it is left to the member associations to do so.

6. Personnel of Secretariat and Categories

The Secretariat consists of 28 employees - 1 chief of the Secretariat, and 10 secretaries or assistants; the rest is made up of technical staff. The size of the Secretariat has increased from 16 in 1977, to 28 in 1980.

7. Budget Size and Contribution Criteria

Total budget for 1979 : Dkr. 7,500,000. Normally, the criteria for contribution payments is 28 Dkr. per member in affiliated organisations, with a small reduction for the large organisations.

II. AIMS AND PRIORITIES

1. Aims and Objectives

The aims and objectives of the FTF are :-

(1) to take care of the common interests of its members in relation to the Folketinget (the parliament), the government, and any other public authority.

(2) to cooperate with other organisations of employees inside and outside the country;

(3) to carry out research into wages and working conditions of its member groups;

(4) to become involved in the negotiations with the employer regarding wages and working conditions, on the request of member organisations; and

(5) to organise civil servants and salaried employees.

2. Policy Priorities

Judging by the information supplied during the interview, it is possible to rank the policy priorities of the FTF in the following manner :-

(a) Very important - employment and vocational guidance
                  (working conditions)
                - economic policy
                - social affairs
                - research, science and education

(b) Important   - competition
                - transport
                - taxation
                - consumer affairs

(c) Occasionally - migrant workers
     important   - banking, credit.

III. CHANNELS OF INFLUENCE (National and EC Level)

1. National Level

The most important channels of influence for the FTF on the national level are as follows, in order of importance :-

    1. Public committees
    2. Government ministries and bureaucracy
    3. Other national interest groups
    4. Parliamentary committees

Through these the FTF has regular contacts with the government administration and national interest groups via oral, personal and written communication and contact. Due to the recognition of the FTF as an equal partner to the LO in labour relations, the FTF is represented in a large number of public committees (1976 : 40; 1978 : 57). This channel of influence is regarded as the most valuable to the FTF, although those committees are, of course, limited to the times when they are actually in session.

The channels available to the FTF on the national level are more important to the organisation than those on the European level. Even issues arising from EC policies will be treated, firstly, on the national level through contacts in the government administration or public committees. Contacts with other interest groups, mainly the LO, have some importance, whereas contacts with parliamentary committees have little, and contacts with political parties or individual members of parliament have, normally, no importance for the FTF.

2. European Level

The most important channels of influence on the European level for the FTF are as follows :-

    1. European interest groups
    2. Advisory committees with national representatives
    3. The Economic and Social Committee

Contacts with these bodies are of a written, personal and oral nature. With all of these bodies the FTF has regular contacts and, occasionally, refers to the European Commission, where personal contacts exist.

The FTF is a member of the ETUC, which it considers to be the most important organisation for its purposes on the European level. The ETUC is the only European interest group to which the FTF belongs. It is the principle aim of the ETUC to promote the interests of employees in relation to the EC authorities. It also acts as a transmitter of information on EC issues to the various national members, and attempts to coordinate the views of these members on EC policy. The FTF, therefore, considers the ETUC as a 'listening post'. However, should a ETUC decision be made that does not conform to FTF views, then the final report of the ETUC will clearly state that the FTF disagrees.

It was stated in the interview that the FTF will not openly work against ETUC decisions, but it is difficult to assess how that can be avoided since, on controversial issues, the member organisations of the FTF are free to make their own assessments and decisions.

Furthermore, the FTF is represented by one member of the Executive Committee on the Economic and Social Committee. The President and some members of the Executive Committee participate in meetings in Brussels three to five times a year. The International Secretary of the FTF participates in such meetings as well.

Two areas of importance on the European level are transport and migrant workers - in all other areas, national channels prevail.

IV. TREATMENT OF COMMUNITY AFFAIRS

FTF has not reorganised its internal organisational structure in relation to the EC in general or specific EC policies as a result of the Danish entry into the Community. There is no special office or coordinating committee to deal with such issues.

However, international activities of the FTF increased with the Danish entry to the EC, as it joined the ETUC and the Nordic Trade Union Confederation (NFS), (established in 1973 and 1972, respectively), when these organisations were established, in conjunction with the LO. This was, however, only indirectly linked to the Danish entry into the EC.

Increasing international relations prompted the FTF to employ one international secretary who deals with all international questions in relation to the EC, ETUC, NFS, ICFTU, OECD/TUAC, ILO, etc. The international secretary participates in the general meetings, should EC questions arise, and handles all questions, whether economic or organisational, that relate to international activities. Finally, he coordinates the activities of the FTF at EC level in such institutions or committees as the Economic and Social Committee, or the Standing Committee on Employment.

V. RELATIONS WITH EUROPEAN INTEREST GROUPS

FTF joined the ETUC, together with the LO, when the ETUC was established in 1973. ETUC is considered a valuable source of information regarding EC developments and policies and a forum for the exchange of views between different members. As a consequence of joining the organisation, the international activities of the FTF have been expanded. It is the view of the FTF that these international contacts are necessary, particularly in relation to EC policies as, for instance, the efforts to harmonise certain educational programmes, and the training of certain groups, such as nurses or midwives. The specific policies related to these issues are, however, dealt with by the individual member associations concerned.

The operation and positions taken by the ETUC have not, so far, affected the internal cohesion of the FTF. However, given the diversity of interests in the FTF, a cautious approach to ETUC activities has been taken by the FTF. The more controversial issues are not dealt with by the FTF, but its member associations. Should the FTF disagree with ETUC positions, as has been the case in relation to certain educational programmes and the development of the EC institutions, the FTF will make its point of view clear to the ETUC and the final report must clearly state that the FTF disagrees with the position stated (see remarks under European Level).

The membership in the ETUC has not affected the relations between the FTF and the Danish Government in any specific way, although it may be the case that the FTF's position has been strengthened by being able to point to a common position in the ETUC. But, such an approach has not been taken deliberately to obtain a 'better' offer from government. Up to now, it has not occurred that the FTF has withheld information from the government due to a position taken by the ETUC, but such a situation could well arise, given a specific situation.

In controversial issue areas of the ETUC, the member associations of the FTF are free to make their point of view known to the government to secure their own interests.

Sources

FTF Publications - Constitution and Rules : as adopted by the FTF Congress, November, 1978. Congress Reports 1974-76 and 1976-78. Faellesradet, Journal of the FTF, monthly. FTF-International, published, FTF, October 1976.

J. Buksti and L. Norby Johansen, Danske organisationers Hvem-Hvad-Hvor, (Copenhavn : Politikens Forlag, 1977).

Archive on Danish interest organisations, Institute of Political Science, University of Aarhus, Denmark.

C.A. Petersen, 'FTF's dannelse og udvikling', J. Buksti (ed.), Organisationer under forandring, (Aarhus: Politica, 1980).

Interview   Mr. Hans Martens, International Secretary

                 carried out by
                 Mr. Jacob Buksti, 13th May, 1980.

4

Fédération Française des Cadres de la
Fonction Publique (French Federation
of Public Service Staffs)

President : A. Ricco

Sectretary General: M. de Goustine

Address : 30, rue de Gramont
75002 Paris.

Tel. 742.97.43

I. ORGANISATIONAL FEATURES

1. Date of Establishment - 1959.

2. Membership Size

The FFCFP has approximately 20,000 members, which are
grouped in 60 unions, some of these being organised in federations (postal services, cultural affairs, defence, etc).

3. Administrative Bodies

(a) The Federal Congress is composed of representatives
from the federations or national union supporters.
Each delegate to the Congress is mandated for two years;
Congress is convened under normal conditions, once
every two years. In exceptional circumstances, the
President can call an extraordinary congress after
notifying the Federal Committee of this intention.
Congress sets and approves the main policy guidelines
of the FFCFP.

(b) The Federal Committee is the executive organ of
the FFCFP. It oversees the daily working of the FFCFP
and takes initiatives, if necessary, in the areas
designated its responsibility. The Committee meets
every two months.

(c) The Federal Bureau is composed of a president, 4
vice-presidents, 1 secretary general, 1 treasurer, and
8 members. The Bureau is elected by the Federal
Committee. The president elect of the Bureau is, ipso
facto, President of the Federation. The role of the
Bureau is to accomplish all the administrative work of
the Federation required by the statutes or by the implementation of directives made by the Federal Committee.

4. Relationship with Members and Organisational Cohesion

In terms of internal structures, the FFCFP follows the
pattern of most trade union federations in France. It has a
'vertical' system of organisation (federations and craft
unions) and a 'horizontal' one (regional and departmental
sections).

   Disagreements within the FFCFP are mostly of a technical
nature and rarely involve fundamental issues. The FFCFP
publishes a bi-monthly newsletter informing its members of

the activities of the Executive. The Federation also
provides its membership with certain services, such as
pension facilities.

5. Decision-Making Style

Decisions in the Federal Congress can be based on simple
majority and those of the Federal Committee on absolute
majority.

6. Personnel of the Secretariat and Categories

The Federation employs 2 full time, salaried, personnel.

7. Budget Size and Contribution Criteria

No details were provided. Finances for the FFCFP are
obtained from subscription.

II. AIMS AND PRIORITIES

1. Aims and Objectives

The FFCFP exists to study all general economic and social
questions regarding the professional membership, and to be
receptive to interests affecting the Federation, directly or
indirectly. Defence of the collective interests of the
members is a further objective, as is the pursuit of the
realisation of Federation resolutions. The Federation also
exists to represent its members in public sectors, notably
in consultative, statutory and official organs, whether they
are permanent, temporary or seasonal workers, with the
sincere intention of defending their interests through
collaboration. The FFCFP thus attends diverse congresses,
committees or commissions, at which salaries are discussed.
The Federation, further, makes available the results of its
studies when they can be put to useful purposes, and hopes
to create, eventually, unity among all the organisations
representing members of the public service at the regional,
national and international levels. Finally, the FFCFP
exists to implement its role conferred by law and by
Article 16, Chapter 1, Sec.1, Book 3, of the Code de Travail.

2. Policy Priorities

Issues concerning the FFCFP include the following :
external trade, research, science and education, employment
and vocational training, protection of the environment,

energy policies, economic policy, taxation, agriculture and consumer affairs. Of primary importance are research, science and education, employment and vocational training, energy, economic policy, taxation and, more specifically, defence of the public services, conditions and hours of work and positions of 'fonctionnaires'.

On each of the policy issues mentioned, the Federation expresses its demands in numerous forms, e.g. written and oral questions, personal contacts, etc; however, no common programme is presented to government. In the case of external trade and protection of the environment, only written questions are formulated to express the Federation's views; on agricultural issues, oral questions are also formulated. Only in the transport sector are different procedures adopted, depending on the specific policy issue concerned.

All policy sector issues mentioned are defended, primarily, through national channels of influence, although energy and social policy issues are also conducted through the CIF, and research, science and educational affairs, are expressed in a comparative report drafted by the EC.

III. CHANNELS OF INFLUENCE (National and EC Level)

1. National Level

Primary links, in the form of daily union action, are maintained with the parliament and with the government, both independently and in conjunction with the other unions. Representation on parliamentary committees has the next greatest importance, with occasional contacts with political parties and other interest groups being of lesser importance.

2. European Level

Except for the Economic and Social Committee[*] the FFCFP has not developed any direct links at Community level, as it operates through the CIF and through the USEJF (Union Syndicale Européene des Jeunes Fonctionnaires). The nature of the issue will determine the type of link used, e.g. common programme, written or oral questions, personal contacts, etc; no hard and fast rules apply.

---

[*] The FFCFP is linked with the French Confédération Générale des Cadres (CGC) and the latter has one representative in the Economic and Social Committee.

IV. TREATMENT OF COMMUNITY AFFAIRS

The Federation has no special service for dealing with Community or international affairs. Since May 1978, it has been a member of CIF, which represents the FFCFP at the international and Community level. Community affairs are dealt with by the Federation when necessary, and by the Bureau in particular. On the whole, Community affairs are dealt with as internal issues, as it is not easy to separate them from national affairs.

V. RELATIONS WITH EUROPEAN INTEREST GROUPS

The FFCFP considers that the main aims of the CIF should be to harmonise the systems of public service representation in the member countries and record their negative and positive rights (powers). M. Chapuis represents the Federation at CIF meetings, but links are not regular, even though the Federation only has contacts with the Community institutions through the CIF; the FFCFP feels that it is not sufficiently informed of CIF's activities.

Three specific sectors are defended at the Community level through membership of CIF :-

1. Education (on which the Federation has compiled a report);
2. Post and telecommunications; and
3. Youth unemployment in Europe.

The FFCFP is also a member of the Union of European Young Government Officers (EBJ).

Sources

Statutes of the FFCFP, as of 23.10.1977.

FFCFP Publications - 'La place du fonctionnaire dans le nation', 1974
'Revue bimestrielle', nos.88 and 95
'VIIe Congres Fédéral; la verité sur la hierarchie des traitements dans la fonction publique', 1972
Supplément au no.64.

<u>Interview</u>   Mr. A. Ricco, President, and
Mr. C. Chaperis, Deputy Secretary General

carried out by,
Mr. Dan de Vos, February, 1980.

5

Der Deutsche Beamtenbund, DBB

(The German Federation of

Civil Servants)

Chairman : A. Krause

Address : Dreizehnmorgenweg 36
D-5300 Bonn 2.

Tel. (2221) 37697175

I. ORGANISATIONAL FEATURES

1. Date of Establishment

4th December, 1918; re-established in 1949.

2. Membership Size

Approximately 825,000, as of 30th September, 1979.

3. Administrative Bodies

(a) The National Conference is the highest organ of
the DBB and is responsible for laying down guidelines
for DBB overall policy.

The Conference meets every four years, but may be
called to meet if a two-thirds majority in the
National Executive Council decide in favour of such
an extraordinary session. The Conference consists
of the members of the National Executive Council and
representatives of the member associations.

(b) The National Executive Council is responsible
for legal, political, social and employment related
issues, as well as organisational questions and
relations to the media. It decides on the budget
and general resource allocation. It can call committees
and decide over the entry of new members and any
expulsions.

The Council meets two to three times a year. Its
members consist of the National Council and at least
one representative from each of the member associations.
Larger federation members may have more than one
delegate, the number of which is regulated by the
statutes of the Federation.

(c) The National Council deals with routine employment -
political issues, which do not go forward to the
National Executive Council. It administers the budget
and is responsible for the personnel in the Secretariat.
It can call commissions to investigate certain problematic issue areas.

The Council meets at least four times a year, and
consists of 28 members. These are :-

4 members of the Secretariat

11 representatives of the Landesverbände

8 representatives of the Bundesbeamten-verbände

5 representatives of the Bundesfach-verbände,
and delegates from the special DBB associations,
such as DBB Youth.

(d) The National Administration/Secretariat is
responsible for the implementation of policies made
in the above organs. It consists of 3 deputies, and
a chairman, who presides over the Secretariat
(Bundesgeschäftsstelle) which is, in turn, divided
into four divisions dealing with specific policy
areas (see Figure 5.1 at the end for illustration).

The 11 existing committees, commissions, and working
groups serve solely to assist the decision-making
process of the DBB.

4. Decision-Making Style

Voting in the administrative bodies of the DBB is conducted
on a simple majority basis. Parity of votes means
rejection of the motion.

5. Relationship with Members and Organisational Cohesion

The DBB is a federation consisting of 46 member associations. 11 of these are regional/state federations
(Landesverbände), 20 are national occupational associations
(Bundesfachverbände), and 15 are national civil service
associations (Beamtenverbände). Special DBB organisations
are the DBB Youth, the Women's Association, and the
Community of Collective Bargaining Organisations.
A distinguishing feature between these groups is whether
land or federal laws apply in the regulations of working
conditions. The 15 national civil service associations'
working conditions are regulated by federal law; groups
such as postal workers, customs officials, or railwaymen
fall under this category. In contrast, national
occupational associations are groups of civil servants or
public employees whose working conditions are regulated
by land law. Examples of these groups are the police
force, teachers, or forestry workers. Also included in
this category are civil servants, who fall under a

mixture of land and federal law regulations, such as
pensioners and widows. These groups are organised on a
national basis, but are also represented in their respective Landesverband. The latter are federations of all
unionised civil servants in their particular land,
regardless of occupations. There are Landesverbände
corresponding with the number of Länder in the Federal
Republic.

Internal cohesion within the DBB is ensured by the
representation of all member associations by at least
one representative in the National Conference, National
Executive Council, and the National Council. There, the
members are directly involved in the decision-making
process and wage bargaining procedures.

Sometimes disagreements within the DBB emerge over
the coordination of policies for civil servants (Beamte)
on the one hand, and salaried employees/wage earners
in the public sector on the other, since the legal work
regulations for the two groups are different. Most
individual members of the DBB are of the civil servants
category. Generally, however, agreement exists amongst
all categories of DBB membership in policies and
guidelines.

Furthermore, the DBB provides various special services
for its membership. These include an automobile club,
a youth organisation, a women's representation, socio-
economic institutions, such as an insurance scheme, a
travel service, a book club, and a publications bureau.
The DBB also has educational and recreational facilities,
investment and loan schemes open to all individual members.

6. Personnel of the Secretariat and Categories

There are 33 employees, 1 part time worker, and 1 trainee
working in the Secretariat, which is responsible to the
National Administration under the Chairmanship of
A. Krause and his 3 deputies (see Figure 5.1).

7. Budget Size and Contribution Criteria

The total budget is not available for public scrutiny.
Contributions to the DBB are made by the member associations,
according to the size of their individual membership
numbers. Should an association have more than 20,000
members, it may pay directly to the DBB fund, instead of

paying the Landesverband, which channels money to the DBB, as is normal practice.

II. AIMS AND PRIORITIES

1. Aims and Objectives

The aims and objectives of the DBB are laid down under paragraph 3 of the statutes. These are :-

(1) The DBB and its member associations will work together in the interests of their individual members.

(2) It is the objective of the DBB to represent and voice the employment, political, social and legal requirements and needs and interests of their individual members.

(3) The DBB as an overarching trade union organisation will address itself to general social and political questions.

(4) The member associations have the duty to provide the following to their members :-

(a) representation and articulation of employment-political, legal and social needs and interests of their individual members;

(b) representation of the interests of their individual members vis-à-vis the employer;

(c) legal aid and protection in occupational or employment related issues; and

(d) distribution of information of the DBB and its member associations through the appropriate channels.

(5) On request from the member associations the DBB will take responsibility for the duties listed under (4)(a) - (c). Insofar as costs arise, the given member association is bound to reimburse the DBB.

(6) The DBB provides further economic benefits which can be utilised by either the member association or individual members who are bound to reimburse the DBB for any costs.

(7) The individual members can utilise these provisions, according to DBB regulations.

2. Policy Priorities

Judging from the information supplied by the DBB (Interview Scheme p.6), it is possible to rank the policy priorities of the organisation in the following manner :-

(a) Very important - economic and legal position of
  civil servants
  - income and wage policy
  - social security and social policy
  - codetermination and representation
  in the work place

(b) Important - education/vocational guidance
  - asset formation
  - collective bargaining policies
  - internal and external security
  - economic policies
  - taxation

(c) Occasionally - consumer affairs
  important - competition policy
  - environment
  - research, science and education

Stresses on the importance of these issue areas may vary according to the problems facing sections or the organisation of the DBB as a whole at different times and specific circumstances. A certain overlap of these areas is also unavoidable, and the DBB is at pains to point to the linkage between government policies in the economic, social and other fields, and the issues and problem areas facing the DBB as a result of these policies.

During the National Conference of 1979, where policy guidelines were set out for the years 1979-83, priority was given to such questions as the proposed legal reform of public sector working regulations. Topics such as better opportunities of cooperative decision-making and the consolidation of career, incomes and work distribution regulations were also discussed by Conference. The DBB stressed the need to counter critics of the state bureaucracy, who have been demanding a smaller and more efficient state apparatus, by increasing information and communication flows to the general public, thereby explaining the difficulties and improving the relationship between the public and the bureaucracy (Arbeitsprogramm 1979:3).

In terms of incomes policy, the DBB stressed the need for constant adjustment of civil servants' pay to the overall incomes developments, and rejected claims that civil service pay had risen faster than other sections (Arbeitsprogramm 1979:7; Geschäftsbericht 1979:61). Other areas discussed were the working conditions of teachers, where the DBB called for a standardisation of teachers' working hours, as these may vary between the Länder of the Federal Republic (Geschäftsbericht 1979:41/42).

All in all, the DBB discussed well over 25 general and specific topic areas of importance to general, as well as small sections, of DBB membership.

III. CHANNELS OF INFLUENCE (National and EC Level)

1. National Level

The most important areas of influence on the national level are as follows, in order of importance :-

1. Government ministries
2. Individual members of parliament
3. Political parties
4. Parliamentary committees
5. Other public committees

The DBB has regular oral and written contacts with government ministries, political parties, and members of parliament. The DBB entertains some common programmes with these institutions and individuals in order to ensure that its interests are understood and acknowledged. With parliamentary and public committees, the DBB has occasional contact, depending on how important the issue being dealt with by the committee is to the DBB (Interview Scheme p.3/4).

The DBB is, next to the DGB, the only union organisation that is, according to paragraph 94 of the Civil Service Law (Bundesbeamtengesetz), entitled to participate in the preparation of all general regulations as pertaining to the civil service. This entitles the Federation to take part in the creation of civil service working conditions and regulations by the state. However, this right to participate at this level of governmental decision-making does not restrict the DBB's right to attempt to influence public opinion, or to put forward proposals and recommendations of its own to parliament or government.

The channels to the decision-making organs in the Federal Republic are, therefore, not only formally institutionalised but can also be influenced by outside pressure through the media, public opinion, or lobbying in the Bundestag or Bundesrat, and the various political parties. The DBB has its own press and publications office, through which it attempts to inform both its members and the general public via pamphlets, leaflets, and other publications.

2. European Level

The DBB deals with international and European questions through an external relations section of the National Administration/Secretariat. In addition, the DBB has an office in Brussels, employing one part time worker, dealing exclusively with EC issues. Contacts with the EC Commission are made through this office. Personal contacts with members of the European Parliament and its committees and party groups are also maintained. One member of the DBB national administration is a member of the Economic and Social Committee of the EC, and represents the group 'miscellaneous interests' therein. The Chairman of the DBB is the Vice-President of the International Organisation of National and International Public Service Unions (CIF), and regularly participates in their sessions, of which there are usually 7 per year.

A number of DBB member associations (postal, railway, teachers) which belong to various international or European interest group associations, are also represented at the European level. European and international contacts are, therefore, wide, yet not as intensive as those on the national level. According to DBB sources they are, however, to be considered as of growing importance in the future, especially contacts at the European level (Arbeitsprogramm 1979:17).

IV. TREATMENT OF COMMUNITY AFFAIRS

An indication of the growing importance the DBB attaches to the EC can be seen in the establishment of the DBB office in Brussels, near the EC Commission. However, the importance of EC affairs depends, largely, on what policies, if any, are being introduced by the EC institutions. It appears that EC policy decisions have not, so far, conflicted significantly with the interests of the DBB.

With regard to EC activities, the DBB has mainly tried to influence decisions in social policy, employment and vocational guidance, legal regulations of working conditions and tax matters, and education and environmental policy. The DBB has, in conjunction with CIF policy, actively encouraged its members to participate in the direct elections to the European Parliament.

During the DBB National Conference of 1979, some time was devoted to European affairs and, in the resulting work programme, the following proposals were put forward :-

1. To extend supranational activities to strengthen interests and political importance.

2. Foster measures to ensure continued functioning of the public services on the international level.

3. Extend the possibilities to influence decisions at European level.

4. Perpetuate the realisation of trade union pluralism in the European region and especially in the European institutions (Arbeitsprogramm 1979:17).

V. RELATIONS WITH EUROPEAN INTEREST GROUPS

To date, the CIF, so far as the DBB is concerned, has always been able to reach minimal consensus on any policy decision without jeopardising or compromising the DBB, either in relation to its members or the government of the Federal Republic (Questionnaire p.7).

The DBB views the CIF as an organisation that should pursue the following objectives :-

-   recognition of the CIF by the EC

-   structural development of the civil service in view of its growing role in the national, as well as international context

- enforcement of Article 117 of the Treaty of Rome in regard to the civil service

- integration of its member associations (Questionnaire p.9).

Sources

W. Bierfelder - Handwörterbuch des Offentlichen Dienstes
'Das Personalwesen'
Sonderdruck Erich Schmidt Verlag, 1976
Berlin.

Deutscher Beamtenbund Bundesvertretertag -
Geschäftsbericht der Bundesleitung 1975
Geschäftsbericht der Bundesleitung 1979

Deutscher Beamtenbund Bundesleitung : Arbeitsprogramm 1979

Deutscher Beamtenkalender 1979

Sammlung der für den Deutschen Beamtenbund geltenden satzungs-und vertragsrechtlichen Bestimmungen (12. Nov.1975) Vereintliche Verlagsanstalt, Düsseldorf.

Questionnaire and Interview Scheme answered by

Miss M. Hoffman,
Assistant in Division I,
National Secretariat of the DBB, May, 1980.

FIGURE 5.1
Administration of DBB

German Civil Servants Association National Administration
Chairman: A. Krause
Vice-Chairman : K. W. Baetge MdB
Vice-Chairman : U. Berger MdB
Vice-Chairman : K. Klein

National Secretariat
Supervised by A. Krause

Bureau of Secretariat
Supervised by Thea Pakebusch
Assistants: I.Adams, R.Bauer

Press Bureau
Supervision: D. Fengels
Secretariat: T. Pakebusch
Assistant: B. Humpert
1. Press and Public Relations
2. Editing DBB Publications

Cashiers
Supervision : B. Schaaf
- budget membership
- contributions
- publication charges

Division I
Supervised by Dr.U.Röckl
Secretariat: G.Hack
Assistant: M.Hoffman NM

1. Fundamental issues Dr. Röckl
- general social policies
- trends of development in the civil service
- administration and political questions reform policies
- contact to science

2. Communication Dr. Röckl
A) External and Internal Communication
B) Use of external data banks Hoffman
C) Preparation for DBB conference

3. External Relations Individual Social Issues
A) Cooperation with other associations
B) International cooperation Media Environment Hoffman

Division II
Law and Organisation supervised by G. Esser Assistants as below

1. Justice: G. Esser
- constitution regulations
- legal protection

2. Civil Servants Law : V. Klinkhardt
- general civil servants law
- reform of civil servants law
- career rights
- discipline/other areas

3. Organisation:G.Esser H.W. Erlenbüter
- general organisation
- organisational reform
- DBB and member associations

4. International Organisation: G.E. Ber Erlenbüter
A) Personal issues Erlenbüter
B) Information and documentation - E. Hörmlein
C) Technical Services Erlenbüter
- postal services
- telephones
D) Secretariat of Tribunal Erlenbüter

Division III
Pay, Security and Economic Policies supervised by Dr.A.Hölder
Secretariat: I. Woelke

1. Pay : E. Kempf
A) Pay development and law
B) Additional fields : H.D. Reich

2. Civil Servants Social Security and Provisions E. Kempf
- civil servants legal entitlements
- developments of these entitlements

3. Economic Policies Dr. Hölder
- economic policy
- social policy
- tax policy
- self help provisions and economic institutions

Division IV
Education, Codetermination, Representation and Technology Supervisor: Dr. Ilibertz
Secretariat: S. Dolff

1. Codetermination Dr. W. Ilibertz
- public sector
- trends in private sector

2. Representation Dr. W. Ilibertz
- consultation and trends

3. Education: Dr.Ilibertz
- general aims
- school/high school issues
- adult education
- occupational training and further education

4. Technology:Dr.Ilibertz
- coordination between technical and nontechnical public service
- peculiarities of technical civil service

5. Additional areas Dr. Ilibertz
- data protection
- new technology

57

6

Anotate Dioikesis Eneson Demosion Ypallelan
ADEDY (Highest Administration of Civil
Servants Association)

President : Michalis Papacostas

Secretary General : Georgios Bramis

Address :   Lycourgou, 10
            Athens.

            Tel. 32 46109

I. ORGANISATIONAL FEATURES

1. Date of Establishment - 1945.

2. Membership Size

The ADEDY consists of 65 civil servants and public employee unions, comprising approximately 110,000 individual members; its membership is increasing. Member organisations of the ADEDY are :-

- (a) occupational associations;

- (b) national occupational associations;

- (c) occupational associations for members who cannot form appropriate organisations on the higher level; and

- (d) local branch associations.

If there are more than one occupational or local associations representing civil servants, only one of these organisations can join the ADEDY.

3. Administrative Bodies

(a) The Congress is called upon to meet every four years by the General Council and consists of representatives of all member associations. It can only take decisions if one-third of its members are present, and decisions are made on an absolute majority basis. It decides on general policy guidelines. If considered necessary, Congress may be summoned by the General Council or various member associations with at least one-third of the total votes for an extraordinary meeting.

(b) The General Council administers the ADEDY. It consists of 70 members, who are elected by Congress for a period of four years. The body elects a president, two vice-presidents, the general secretary, and a specialised vice-secretary. It meets regularly once a month, and can make decisions if half, less one, of its members are present. Decision-making style is by simple majority vote.

(c) The Executive Council is responsible for the implementation of policies by Congress and the General

Council and application of the statutes. It consists of 15 members, who are elected by the General Council from within its members. The Executive Council elects a president, 3 vice-presidents, 1 general secretary, 1 vice-general secretary, 1 specialised secretary, and a cashier. It meets twice a month.

(d) The Control Committee supervises the financial affairs of the ADEDY. It consists of 5 members and 5 deputy members who are elected by Congress. These members also belong to the General Council but do not have any voting rights in this Council. It elects one chairman, meets once a month, and can make decisions if 3 of its members are present. It presents a report to the General Council once a year, and presents the Congress with a financial statement of the ADEDY affairs every four years.

(e) The ADEDY also has a Publications Committee which consists of 3 members elected by the General Council and is responsible for ADEDY publications. The Publications Committee releases a newspaper every two weeks.

(f) There is also a Disciplinary Committee consisting of the President and General Secretary of the Executive Council, the President and General Secretary of the General Council, and the Chairman of the Control Committee. The Chairman is the President of the Executive Council.

4. Decision-Making Style

Decisions at the Congress level can only be taken by absolute majority. An exception is made in relation to questions concerning the statutes, where any changes require a three-quarters majority, and can only be made by Congress. The last such change was undertaken in 1971, although another change in regulations was proposed in 1979, and is currently being considered by the appropriate Athenian court.

5. Relationship with Members and Organisational Cohesion

The members are elected by the General Council to staff an Organisational Committee which assures the smooth running of the organisation and its relations with member affiliates. Disciplinary action within the ADEDY is taken by the Disciplinary Committee. Thus, the ADEDY's internal cohesion is not only ensured by the representation of each member association within the administrative bodies, but also

through the function of the organisation to act as inter-
mediary amongst its members in relation to sensitive issues.
Once decisions have been taken by the administrative bodies,
the member associations of the ADEDY are bound to adhere to
them. Furthermore, they have to report their financial
position and activities to the central bodies every six
months.

6. Personnel of the Secretariat and Categories

Two members of staff.

7. Budget Size and Contribution Criteria

ADEDY's budget was 2,500,000 Drachmen in 1980 (about
42,000 ECU). The ADEDY budget is made up by :-

- entrance fees from the member associations

- contributions by the member associations which are
  calculated on the number of individual members and
  are payable every three months

- voluntary contributions which are set on a yearly
  basis by the General Council

- extraordinary contributions which are set by the General
  Council and are binding on the member associations

- gifts, inheritances and proceeds from various functions

- interest emanating from the associations' funds.

II. AIMS AND PRIORITIES

1. Aims and Objectives

The aim of the ADEDY is to promote the role and function of
civil servants, to improve the cultural and material position
of its members, and to protect their occupational interests.
To realise these aims, the ADEDY pursues the following
objectives :-

(1) promote the spirit of collectivity and solidarity
amongst civil servants, and present a united and disci-
plined front in respect to other union organisations on
higher levels;

(2) entry of all civil servants into the local and occupational associations and incorporation of these groupings
into the ADEDY;

61

(3) inform civil servants through seminars, meetings, festive occasions, publications, books and pamphlets; and

(4) cultivate and make available the intellectual, moral and material potential of the public service.

2. Policy Priorities

Next to the aims set out in the statutes of the Association, the general policy priorities of the organisation can be exemplified by the report put out by the 24th National Congress in 1979, which sets out the main achievements and activities during the period 1975 to 1979. General policy areas in which the Association had been successful, were :-

- the introduction of a new incomes distribution table for civil servants and public employees in the legal services, which had become of utmost importance after the re-establishment of a democratic regime in Greece

- reorganisation of the hierarchy amongst civil servants and their functions and the favourable solution of problems connected with this reorganisation

- a visible improvement of the pension scheme

- regulation of working hours and holidays

- regulation of the right to strike by civil servants which had been planned in the Constitution of 1975.

Other activities of the ADEDY included :-

- proposals for changes in the tax structure and measures to combat inflation, both of which were presented to the government

- attempts to improve the working regulations of the social security funds and administration of its fixed and moveable assets

- proposed improvements of the health sector and in the area of distribution of medical services

- activities in connection with the special problems of the social, economic and cultural nature of civil servants, as well as their unionisation

- proposals to government for the reorganisation and modernisation of the civil bureaucracy, so that it can adequately deal with the increasing demands placed upon it at the national level, as well as new challenges to the public service due to entry into the EC.

On the international level, the ADEDY stressed the need for international cooperation and upheld and extended contacts with trade union organisations in both Eastern and Western Europe. A special area of concern are contacts with a similar public service union in Cyprus, with whom the ADEDY has increased relations.

III. CHANNELS OF INFLUENCE (National and EC Level)

1. National Level

The ADEDY is represented by its President in the Economic and Social Council (SKOP). The most frequent and important channel for pursuing ADEDY's interests are government ministries.

2. European Level

The growing importance of the EC is reflected in the demands for a modernised and better organised civil service due to the demands placed upon it by entry into the EC. Contacts with the EC are maintained via their representation in the Economic and Social Committee (two members) and EC Advisory Committees, and their membership in the European Trade Union Public Service Committee (ETUPSC).

IV. TREATMENT OF COMMUNITY AFFAIRS

Since Greece only became a member of the EC in January 1981, it may be as yet somewhat early to judge the importance of EC influences on the Greek civil service, but there can be little doubt that the EC is deemed to be an important factor. Entry into the EC was regarded as a positive measure by the Association.

V. RELATIONS WITH EUROPEAN INTEREST GROUPS

The ADEDY is a member of the European Trade Union Public Service Committee (ETUPSC), but not of any other European trade union federation. Next to its contacts with the ETUPSC, the ADEDY entertains links with individual national trade union organisations, such as the public service unions in Italy and, very importantly, similar organisations in Cyprus. The ADEDY also has links with Eastern European trade union organisations, such as the Hungarian Union Organisation, with whom it has a common programme to enlarge future cooperation. The ADEDY also sent a delegation to the meeting of civil service unions of Eastern Europe, which took place in Warsaw in 1977, and has held various meetings in Athens in which a number of East and West European trade unions took part.

Sources

ADEDY publishes a bimensual journal :

> Statut
> Bilan d'activités de ADEDY 1975-79
> Response to Questionnaire of ESC

Returned Questionnaire

See also General Secretariat of the Economic and Social Committee, the Economic and Social Interest Groups of Greece. Documentation, Editions Delta, Brussels 1981, pp. 103-112.

7

The Local Government and Public
Services Union (LGPSU)

President : Vincent Miller

General Secretary : Harold O'Sullivan

Address : 9 Gardiner Place,
Dublin 1.

I.   ORGANISATIONAL FEATURES

1.   Date of Establishment

The LGPSU was established in 1900.

2.   Membership Size

The LGPSU has approximately 16,000 members (1980).

3.   Administrative Bodies

(a)   The Annual Conference is the highest decision-making organ of the union and the guidelines for union policies are made at this level.

(b)   The Executive Board manages and administers the affairs of the organisation when the Annual. Conference is not in session. Meetings are held monthly.

(c)   Divisional Organisations, of which there are two :   the 'Local Government and Public Bodies Division' and the 'Health and Welfare Division'. These bodies mirror the union as a whole and have annual conferences and executive boards of their own, which meet once every three months.   Their existence is to facilitate the management of diverse interests within the union body and membership.

(d)   Branches are responsible for the day to day issues that are of concern to the members.   They are organised along sectoral lines, i.e. common employer, workplace, or vocation.   Each branch must not have less than 100 members.

Branches must meet at least once a month and decisions are taken along simple majority voting lines.

Information supplied by the union Secretariat seems to imply that working groups or committees on specific problematic issue areas are not utilised until absolutely necessary.   The union is small enough for the Secretariat to maintain personal contacts and operate efficiently by the personal contacts and involvement of these officials.   The General Secretary,

66

in particular, believes that committees are a burden
to the organisation, and any committees that are
formed are only constructed on an 'ad hoc' basis.

4.   Decision-Making Style

The Annual Conference takes decisions by simple majority
vote. The Executive Board decides, usually by consensus,
but should this be unobtainable, simple majority voting
prevails. Generally, branches use majority decision-
making procedures.

5.   Relationship with Members and Organisational Cohesion

The union is a multi grade union representing local
authority engineers, technicians, vocational groups and
health authority staff. The latter group is particularly
important, due to the huge involvement of the state in
the health service.

There are no ideological problems within the union,
which represents supporters from all parties of the Irish
political system, and there are no fundamental policy or
goal problems.

Any problems of cohesion that may occur are due to the
constant jockeying for position by the diverse groups
the union represents.

Contacts between the executive and members are maintained
through the branch structure, as well as the administrative
body representatives. Since the membership of the union
is relatively small, it is also possible for the members
of the Secretariat to keep in personal contact with a
great proportion of the membership. From all accounts,
this system seems to adquately cover the needs of the
union.

The union publishes a newspaper which specifically aims
at informing the membership of details relating to their
employment. It does not distribute any further general
information.

6.   Personnel and Categories of the Secretariat

The LGPSU has 17 full time staff, as follows :-

          1   General Secretary

          1   Deputy General Secretary

          5   Assistant General Secretaries (Regional)

          1   Financial Secretary

          1   Health Services Officer

          8   secretarial staff

7. Budget Size and Contribution Criteria

The LGPSU's total budget for 1979 was £200,000. All
members are full members and pay their contribution fee
to the local branch, which contributes a set amount to
central funds, as well as withholding a certain proportion
of the fees for local activities.

II. AIMS AND PRIORITIES

1. Aims and Objectives

According to the statutes of the union,

" The objects of the union are to improve the conditions
and protect the interests of the members; to regulate
the relations between its members and their employing
public bodies; to assist the movements for the betterment
of industrial conditions; to assist its members when
unemployed; to protect its members from social, sectarian,
racial, sex or other forms of unfair discrimination; to
establish a fund or funds for any purpose approved by the
union; and to these ends adopt the following methods :-

(a)   the provision of legal assistance in connection
      with any or all of the above objects;

(b)   the safeguarding of its members' interests in
      connection with legislative measures and the
      securing of effective administration of existing
      laws which may affect the general and material
      welfare of its members; and

(c)   the adoption of any other legal methods which
      may be deemed advisable in the interests of the
      members."

For the purpose of promoting these objectives and of
making these methods effective, the union may aid and join

with other unions or other societies, or federations of unions and societies, in Ireland.

2. Policy Priorities

These only exist in terms of national issues and any European aspects are purely incidental.

Social affairs are the most frequently represented policy area and this is largely in connection with the effects of these policies on the workers the union represents.

Economic policy is the next most important area of interest representation due to the role of the ICTU in negotiations with the government and the FUE (Federated Union of Employers). Ireland has seen a series of nationally negotiated pay agreements and economic policy of the government is heavily influenced by this. At the time of writing, negotiations were in progress for reaching a 'national understanding' in the economic field and the LGPSU is heavily involved in these negotiations.

After these issues, the question of research, science and education, protection of the environment, and agriculture, would be of more or less equal standing. This is due to the representation of workers by the union who are indirectly or directly involved in those areas (e.g. vocational and educational departments of local authorities, sanitary engineers, health officials, and local agricultural advisory services).

Areas on external affairs and consumer policy come last on the list. Consumer policy is only relevant in the wider context of economic policy.

External affairs are concerned with Third World affairs and a fund has been established (£8,000 - 4 per cent of the annual budget) for relief work and is allocated in conjunction with the Department of Foreign Affairs. This is a new development in union policy and was adopted at the last Annual Conference, and is still at an elementary stage. As yet, there are no European aspects to this development but there may be, according to the General Secretary, some new initiatives in this area.

III. CHANNELS OF INFLUENCE (National and EC Level)

1. National Level

The most frequent dealings of the LGPSU are with the
government bureaucracy and the lobbying of ministers. Of
next greatest importance are contacts with other unions
and the ICTU (Irish Congress of Trade Unions). Contacts
are made as often as necessary, and take the form of
personal contacts (given the smallness of the Irish
system), as well as formally written or oral requests.
Contacts with public committees are rare but, nevertheless,
entertained. Political parties and MPs are not considered
important (despite ICTU affiliation to the Irish Labour
Party) as major channels of influence on legislation.

2. European Level

Not of any relevance and any such contacts are maintained
through the ICTU or the ETUC.

(See Treatment of EC Affairs for further information).

IV. TREATMENT OF EC AFFAIRS

(General remarks : the EC has little or no effect on Irish
groups outside agriculture. Questions relating to
European aspects are only of little relevance to concerned
parties. Problems are seen as local and of no great
interest to the 'greater European ideal').

Indications are that the LGPSU has not been affected by
the European perspective. Any problems that may arise are
handled by the General Secretary or, if important, by the
Executive Board.

There has been no increase in staff numbers due to
European affairs and, also, no reallocation of duties.
The European perspective has had no very direct effects
on the interests, aims and objectives of the union, and
has not directly affected its activities.

The LGPSU is indirectly affiliated to the European Trade
Union Confederation (ETUC) through the ICTU. The LGPSU's
main dealings with the European questions are, in terms
of its membership, in the Irish Congress of Trade Unions
(ICTU) and the particular stance taken by this
organisation. The idea of using European pressure groups

as an instrument of influence on the national government, or of attempting to influence EC legislation through the ICTU is of no relevance to this union.

V. RELATIONS WITH EUROPEAN INTEREST GROUPS

The LGPSU is affiliated to the European Trade Union Public Services Committee (ETUPSC). It is also indirectly affiliated to the European Trade Union Confederation (ETUC) through its membership of the Irish Trade Union Congress (ICTU).

Sources   Statutes of the LGPSU.

Interview   Mr. Harold O'Sullivan,
                 General Secretary of the LGPSU

                 carried out by,
                 Mr. Bill Beamish, November 1980.

8

Federazione fra le Associazioni e i Sindicati
Nazionale dei Quadri Direttivi della Funzione
Pubblica DIRSTAT (Federation of the Association
& National Trade Union of Higher Civil Servants)

Secretary General : Professor Saverio Vestri

Address :   Via Plinio 21
            Rome.

            Tel. 380991-381516

I. ORGANISATIONAL FEATURES

1. Date of Establishment

October, 1948.

2. Membership Size

DIRSTAT has approximately 11,000 members. It lost a number of members through the early retirement scheme of higher civil servants in 1973 but has, however, been able to regain numbers through the creation of a division for pensioners.

3. Administrative Bodies

(a) The National Congress is the highest decision-making body of DIRSTAT. Its decisions are binding on all member associations and their individual members. Congress decides on overall policy strategy, and on statutes and changes therein. Congress also elects the 25 members of the Central Executive Council, the Budget Committee, and the Referee in the Tribunal. It meets, generally, every four years.

(b) The General Council is the highest decision-making body when Congress is not in session. Its decisions are binding for the member associations. It coordinates the actions taken by the Association, and discusses any issues that have not been dealt with at Congress. The General Council consists of the chairmen of each member association, the members of the Central Executive Council, and members who have been former presidents or general secretaries of DIRSTAT. Usually, the General Council meets in May, except for the years when the National Congress is in session.

(c) The Central Executive Council is the 'governing' body of DIRSTAT. The Executive Council is responsible for implementation of policies laid down by Congress. It investigates special problems experienced by individual member unions and tries to find solutions through consultation, commissions, committees and working groups. The Executive Council meets, usually, every two months.

(d) The Executive Commission is responsible for implementation of policies and meets, generally, once a month. It consists of 9 members who are elected by the Central Executive Council and include, amongst others, the General Secretary, the newspaper director (Editor), and the Chairman of the Legal Service.

(e) General Secretariat - the General Secretary represents the Federation in all aspects, and is the Chairman of the Central Executive Council and the Executive Commission. He supervises the work of the General Secretariat, in which the administrative secretary, the newspaper director, and the legal advisors are employed. He employs staff and supervises spending and income.

(f) The Budget Committee - this committee consists of 3 members and 2 deputies. Its function is to examine the financial position of the organisation and put it forward to the Central Executive Council, with whom it has to consult over size, and obtain advice, as well as the National Congress.

(g) Tribunal/Referee - the Tribunal/Referee of DIRSTAT has 3 members and 2 deputies, and is summoned by the General Secretary to solve controversial issues that have not been adequately dealt with by the other administrative bodies.

(h) Commissions - the number of commissions, committees and working groups vary according to needs as perceived by DIRSTAT. DIRSTAT also participates in official government commissions, such as Consiglio Superiore de la Pubblica Amministrazione - the highest council for the public service - which is responsible for guidelines at the High School for Public Administration. DIRSTAT also participates in the administration of the Ministry of Justice, Ministry of Defence, Ministry for Foreign Trade, Ministry of Health, and the Chancery.

4. Decision-Making Style

All of the above administrative bodies take decisions through simple majority voting. In case of parity, the party with whom the Chairman has voted will be superior. In cases of changes in the constitution, a majority of two-thirds is required.

5. Relationship with Members and Organisational Cohesion

Regional Unions represent DIRSTAT in each region and
regulate relations between region and head office. The
regional council consists of members of the Central
Executive Council of the provincial associations, and
elects one secretary. In every province DIRSTAT has one
provincial union, which coordinates provincial and national
policies. The Provincial Council consists of as many
members as there are DIRSTAT member associations in the
province. It elects one provincial secretary, a vice-
secretary, and a budget supervisor from its members.

DIRSTAT consists solely of higher civil servants and,
therefore, is able to concentrate on the representation of
specific rather than diverse interests of its members.
As a consequence, there are no differences over fundamental
issues. Frequent meetings in the administrative bodies,
as well as simple majority voting in decision-making of
these bodies, promote cooperation and cohesion among its
33 affiliated member organisations. If contentious issues
arise from or among member organisations, a tribunal
within DIRSTAT is called upon to deal with difficulties.
To promote information between DIRSTAT and its members, a
newspaper is regularly published.

6. Personnel of the Secretariat and Categories

The Secretariat of DIRSTAT has 13 full time and 3 part time
staff employees. Also working, are a few pensioners, who
are not paid. The breakdown is as follows :-

1 General Secretary

2 Vice Secretaries

1 Director of Division

1 Director responsible for the newspaper

1 Director of the legal section

1 Administrative Secretary

2 Dirigenti Superiori who are members of the
Executive Commission

1 Prefect as representative of pensioners

2 Direttori Aggiunti

1 Director (for diverse sections)

7. Budget Size and Contribution Criteria

DIRSTAT had a budget of 100 million Lire in 1980.
Contribution size of member associations depends on their
size of membership.

II. AIMS AND PRIORITIES

1. Aims and Objectives

DIRSTAT has the following aims and objectives :-

(1) to represent the wishes, the legal and economic
interests of the higher civil servants, be they active
or retired;

(2) to better the conditions of employment of the
higher civil service and suit the administration to the
needs of the nation; and

(3) to foster the cultural and social interests of its
members.

DIRSTAT is independent and not tied to any political
party.

2. Policy Priorities

The following policy sectors are regarded by DIRSTAT as
important (in list of priority) :-

- Employment policies and vocational guidance and
    education
- Social policies
- Taxation
- Economic policies
- Associational policies
- Consumer interests
- Banking, savings and credit policies
- Research, science and educational policies
- Industrial policies
- Foreign trade

III. CHANNELS OF INFLUENCE (National and EC Level)

Representation of interests is conducted entirely through
national channels.

1. National Level

DIRSTAT has daily contacts and common programmes with government and the ministerial bureaucracy. With the governing parties DIRSTAT has regular and personal contacts. With political parties, parliamentary committees, MPs and other public institutions, DIRSTAT has only occasional contact, mostly in written or oral form, but sometimes through personal contacts.

2. European Level

Except for its previous membership in CIF, DIRSTAT has not used any European channels for exerting influence.

IV. TREATMENT OF COMMUNITY AFFAIRS

Although the members of DIRSTAT are well informed of European issues, and show some interest in them these issues are not dealt with in DIRSTAT. The administrative bodies of DIRSTAT do not provide guidelines on European issues. Individual members may have contacts with European authorities or are actively involved, but not because of their membership in DIRSTAT.

V. RELATIONS WITH EUROPEAN INTEREST GROUPS

DIRSTAT was a member of CIF but, in 1975, asked to withdraw. The prime reasons for withdrawing were that CIF, as an organisation, represented a conglomeration of interests from federal state to local public employees, whereas DIRSTAT represents a much more specialised sector of the civil service. Since DIRSTAT is concerned only with its higher civil servants' members, it was felt that CIF could not pursue DIRSTAT's interests with rigour and effectiveness at the European level.

For DIRSTAT, a representative European interest group should have the following aims and objectives : Standardisation and integration of the constitutions of the public services in the EC member nations, with a clear demarcation of the rights and position of civil servants. This would entail inclusion of all possible international organisations such as the ILO (International Labour Organisation) which would give governments guidelines, to avoid the civil service always being penalised.

Sources

DIRSTAT Publications - Reforma Amministrativa
                      (newspaper series)
                      Azioni Direttiva (newspaper series)

DIRSTAT Statutes

Interview   Professor Francesco Saverio Vestri,
                 Secretary General of DIRSTAT

                 carried out by,
                 Dr. Bruno du Ban on 24th January, 1980.

9

Confédération Générale de la Fonction
Publique, Luxembourg (General
Confederation of Public
Services of Luxembourg)

President : F. Masson

Secretary General : J. Daleiden

Address : 11 Ave de Porte neuve
Luxembourg.

Tel. 00352-20775
00352-33 86 75

I. ORGANISATIONAL FEATURES

1. Date of Establishment

The CGFP has developed over the past seventy years. It was born from the Cooperative des Agents Publics which was initially formed in 1905. In 1909, an autonomous organisation, representing vocational interests of persons employed by the state, was formed with the name Association Général des Fonctionnaires (AGF). After liberation in 1944/45, the AGF was reformed, and in 1966/67, the Confédération Générale de la Fonction Publique (CGFP) was created after a period of crisis, comprising a replacement for the AGF and symbolising a spectacular rebirth of the union of state employees.

2. Membership Size

The CGF comprises 12,700 members. The membership has risen dramatically since 1909, when it had 4,300 members, yet the number of public service sectors has not been increased.

3. Administrative Bodies

(a) The Congress is the highest decision-making body and adopts the programme of action for the CGFP. It meets, primarily, whenever essential questions arise.

(b) The Committee Conference exists in the administrative hierarchy between the Federal Board and Congress. This is the forum where all member organisations can put forward their proposals for the programme. The Conference is composed of delegates from each of the member organisations.

(c) The Federal Board takes all decisions in the name of the CGFP and comprises representatives of affiliated organisations. The Board is composed of 25 persons. It meets six times a year, and decisions are made by absolute majority rule except in matters of essential importance, which have to be considered by all associations, and are decided by unanimity.

(d) The Executive Board exists to execute the decisions of the Federal Board; it is composed of six members :-

1 President

1 General Secretary

2 Vice Presidents

2 members

It meets weekly, and simple majority rule applies.

(e) The Control Commission deals with financial problems, supervision, etc.

(f) The Structural Committees - each public service sector is represented by sectoral committees; thus, each professional group organises and speaks for itself, but with the cap of the CGFP; the CGFP, accordingly, acts as a confederation of the sectoral committees. Thus, the members' interests can be represented without fear of discrimination against one sector in favour of another. Decisions of the committees are taken in line with the Federation's programme.

4. Relationship with Members and Organisational Cohesion

The CGFP groups 32 sub organisations by categories (university personnel, executives, clerical and manual workers), or by sectors (postal services, education, police, etc). Relations with the members are maintained through publication of a detailed bi-monthly newspaper, although this does not report on the Community and international level activities of the CGFP. The newspaper has a circulation of 14,000. The Federation also provides the members with numerous services, including insurance schemes, cheap loan schemes for house purchase, tourist package deals, etc.

A potential source of division among the members is avoided by the use of a committee structure to represent the views and demands of the separate professional bodies included in the CGFP's membership. The main issue of contention among the membership, as referred to above, lies at the personal level of career aspirations.

5. Personnel of the Secretariat and Categories

The Secretariat of the CGFP has 3 full time staff members. (There is also an arrangement whereby the CGFP can call

upon the government civil service to release
'fonctionnaires' for certain tasks).

6. Budget Size and Contribution Criteria

The annual budget is, at present, approximately 3 million
Francs, which is obtained from subscription - 250 Francs
per member, per annum.

7. Decision-Making Style

The CGFP adopts a unanimity voting principle and tends
to present unanimous opinions, embodying a degree of
compromise, rather than majority opinions.

II. AIMS AND PRIORITIES

1. Aims and Objectives

The CGFP exists, primarily, to defend and promote the
interests of the public service and their employees.
More specifically, the role of the organisation is not
merely vis-à-vis the employer. The public service
official has always to defend fiercely his individuality
and is not coincidental with his hierarchial or
administrative position, which is promoting united action.

However, the changing society, especially since the
second World War, has been accompanied by a maturing of a
forecful union movement in the public service sectors.
Thus, the CGFP has developed specific functions as it
has enlarged its membership and scope of action. These
include, taking an important role in the centralisation
and coordination of all the interests and demands of one
or other of the associate members, together with acting as
arbitrator in disputes involving these members. Finally,
the CGFP must be considered as one of the four unions
involved in drafting the national plan, and as an interlocutor for the state on all questions and measures of
general concern to the employees of the state.

2. Policy Priorities

Of primary importance to the Confederation are economic
policy, banking and credit, taxation, social affairs,
employment and vocational training, and protection of the
environment. Of less importance are research, science
and education, and consumer affairs.

III. CHANNELS OF INFLUENCE (National and EC Level)

On the whole, in all policy sectors mentioned, except
that of banking and credit, the Confederation predominantly
uses national channels. In the exceptional case, European
and national channels of influence are of equal importance.

1. National Level

Of most importance are links with government ministries,
then MPs and political parties, followed by links with
parliamentary committees and, finally, access to
government administration. Regular contacts are maintained
with government ministries, parliamentary committees and
MPs. The common action programme is sent to ministerial
departments, together with written and oral questions,
which are also addressed to parliamentary committees and
MPs. However, demands directed at the government
administration are only addressed as oral questions.

And yet, by far the strongest link at the national
level is through the 'sub parliament' representing the
public service sectors. The CGFP is politically
independent, thus it maintains equally good relations with
governments and politicians of all political persuasions.
However, due to the small size of the Luxembourg government,
the CGFP can be directly involved in decisions of both
specific interest to their members and, with the other
three major unions, in developing the government's general
policy of economic and social affairs, etc. Thus, the
CGFP has established a sophisticated network of both
formal and informal links at the national level. Formally,
through the 'sub parliament' and, informally, through the
fact that many of their members - but not members of the
Executive Board - are leading political figures. For
example, the President of the Parliament is a member of
the CGFP, and the Minister of Public Services is both a
member and a Committee delegate.

Links with Luxembourg members of the European Parliament
are also maintained, but from the national, rather than
the Community level.

2. European Level

All relations with Community institutions are conducted
through the CIF; the CGFP has no direct contacts of its
own. This is partly because EC policy has not affected

the interests of the Confederation's members, as was
anticipated at the time the CIF was established and thus
the international organisation has been sufficiently
capable of dealing with the few issues of concern to the
CGFP emanating from Community policies. Secondly, the
CGFP feels that each national public service union should
conduct its affairs within the Community through the CIF
as a matter of principle, as this procedure will produce
the strongest possible voice for European public service
unions.

Community policy, as such, is not dealt with via national
level contacts, as the lack of policy affecting the public
sector has not, as yet, required the use of such links.
However, when the need arises, the CGFP has well developed
communication links with government ministries, government
administration, parliamentary committees, MPs and
political parties, which it will readily use.

IV. TREATMENT OF COMMUNITY AFFAIRS

These and international affairs are dealt with by the
Executive Board, which has a small specialised department
to deal with policies emanating from the Community. A
specialised coordinating committee was also established,
but this did not warrant the employment of extra staff,
as the number of Community policies of importance to the
Confederation is minimal.

V. RELATIONS WITH EUROPEAN INTEREST GROUPS

The CGFP, itself, is only a member of CIF, although some
of its members belong to other specialised international
or Community organisations, e.g. police, postmen.
However, no conflict of purpose or representation arises
from this situation, as CIF represents more general issues,
and will serve as a channel for the representation of
specialised interests, if required to so do.

Membership of CIF has not affected the functioning of
the Confederation or its relations with the national
government. Neither can membership be said to have had an
effect on the internal cohesion of the Confederation. In
fact, on no occasion have the policies of the CIF and those
of the CGFP conflicted.

European integration is thought to be promoted through
membership of CIF, as is the defence of the public services

and their members. Although the CIF is not used to a great extent to influence draft legislation in the Community, membership has provided members of the CGFP with certain experiences which have been used to safeguard and protect the Confederation's members' interests in Luxembourg, regularly.

The CGFP was one of the founder members of CIF, which was expected to promote the uniting of Europe, provide a means for information exchange, and establish contacts between the members of the organisation. It was also intended to influence Community institutions and observe and review the impact of Community legislation on members in the various national contexts, and to represent public service unions at the ILO in Geneva.

However, CIF has not developed as anticipated, in much the same way that the Communities have not become what it was hoped they would be. A number of factors together explain this : lack of Community policy regarding this sector, a certain reluctance to encourage the EC to legislate in a sector which is traditionally regarded as the concern of national governments, the absence of a secretariat in Brussels, and a certain degree of feet dragging on the part of some members of the organisation regarding full and active participation in its activities.

From the point of view of the CGFP, membership of CIF has brought greater contacts with public service unions in other member countries, especially the German members. Contacts with the French organisation have certainly been strengthened through the CIF, and this is possibly the CIF's greatest success so far.

The President of the CGFP is the permanent representative to the CIF.

Sources

Die Kammer der Beamten und Angestellten des öffentlichen Dienstes, Luxembourg (1974).

CGFP : Responses on Questionnaire of the Bureau International du Travail (1975).

CGFP : Programme d'action à moyen terme, December 1977.

Le Programme de la CGFP, December 1977.

CGFP : 70e anniversaire du mouvement syndical de la
fonction publique (1980).

Interview   M. Fernand Masson,
                 President

                 M. Joe Dalaiden,
                 Secretary General

                 M. Erpelding,
                 Delegate of Conference Committee

                 carried out by,
                 Ms. Jane A. Sargent, 30.6.1980.

10

Ambtenarencentrum AC
Civil Service Centrum

Voorzitter (Chairman) : Dr. F. J. Roefs

Secretaris (Secretary) : G. Kenemans

Address : Laan van Meerdervoort 50
NL 2517AM DEN HAAG

Tel. 070/46 93 42

I. ORGANISATIONAL FEATURES

1. Date of Establishment

30th July, 1945.

2. Membership Size

The Ambtenarencentrum has 20 affiliated organisations
which, together, had 105,649 individual members at
1st January, 1979.

3. Administrative Bodies

(a) The General Assembly is the highest administrative
organ of the Ambtenarencentrum. It lays down general
policy and decides on 'all important affairs where the
common interests of administrative personnel are
involved'.

In addition to the Chairman and Secretary, the
General Assembly consists of representatives of the
affiliated associations, each of which has at least two
representatives and two alternates.

(b) The Executive Committee (Het Hoofdbestuur)
prepares meetings of the General Assembly and carries
out the latter's decisions. It is charged with the
direction of the general business of the Ambtenarencentrum, particularly where the statutes or standing
orders do not require a decision by the General
Assembly. It appoints the members of the Management
Committee (dagelijks bestuur) from among its own
membership. The Executive Committee meets monthly.

(c) The Management Committee (Het dagelijks bestuur)
consists of the Chairman, the Secretary, and two
representatives of each of the four 'sectors' into
which the member organisations are divided (i.e.
civilian state personnel, military personnel, local
government and education). It meets at least twice a
month, except during the summer.

There is a permanent committee for budget control
and another, the 'Werkcommissie', that consists of
career people for the various affiliated unions. This
committee advises on policy. There are also a number
of ad hoc committees.

The advice of these committees is of great
importance, although the official organs of the
Ambtenarencentrum take the final decision.

4. Decision-Making Style

All administrative bodies of the Ambtenarencentrum take
decisions by majority vote, unless the statutes specify
otherwise (i.e. in the case of amendments to the statutes,
which require a three-quarter's majority in the General
Assembly).

5. Relationship with Members and Organisational Cohesion

Ambtenarencentrum is not a direct membership organisation;
rather, it is a federation of 20 different organisations
of various sizes and representing various groups. The
smallest of these is the Nederlands Genootschap van
Fysiotherapie (Netherlands Physiotherapy Association)
with 325 members, and the largest is the Central van
Rijkspersoneel ('Centre' of state personnel) with over
25,000 members. Other principal affiliated organisations
include the Netherlands Union of Communal (i.e. local
government) Officials with 13,520 members, the Netherlands
Association of Teachers with 16,629 members, and the
Union of Naval Seamen and ex-Seamen with 14,420 members.

In principle, the defence of those interests which all
public servants have in common, or which concern the
members of more than one affiliated organisation, are
handled by the Ambtenarencentrum. The protection of the
personal interests of their members on the other hand is
wholly reserved to the affiliated organisations. So,
when the individual interests of a member must be
protected before an administrative court, for example,
the Ambtenarencentrum has no jurisdiction.

Between these general and personal categories there is,
of course, a large number of matters which are of direct
concern only to a particular category of public servant.
When all those affected belong to a single affiliated
organisation, that organisation, after consultation with
Ambtenarencentrum, handles the matter. If not, then
Ambtenarencentrum does.

On the question of sensitive issues leading to disagreement within the Ambtenarencentrum, Mr. Kenemans said
that there were two 'streams' within the union, the

'hawks' and the 'doves'. From time to time these 'streams' oppose each other over policy implementation. The first wants to take the way of action and strikes, the other the way of consultation and discussion with the government. The second stream has the upper hand within the Ambtenarencentrum.

Another important issue is whether the Ambtenarencentrum should widen its concerns to become a real trade union 'centre' (vakcentrale) so that other public employees (1) could affiliate to it. Although this issue is still not settled, it has resulted in a modification of the statutes.

To date, such sensitive issues have always resulted in large majorities for any decisions taken, so they have not been as decisive as they might have been. Voting figures are published in the minutes, but the minority position has never, to date, been carried into the open outside the General Assembly.

Frequently, of course, no votes are necessary, since a clear majority for a particular standpoint is obvious.

6. Personnel of the Secretariat and Categories

The Ambtenarencentrum has a staff of 7 at its headquarters, 6 of whom are full time, and 1 is part time. These staff are divided into the Secretariat under the direction of the Secretary, Mr. Kenemans, and the Administration.

7. Budget Size and Contribution Criteria

Total budget for 1979 was Hfl. 1,377,598. Practically all of this money came from affiliation fees, i.e. Hfl. 1,152,037.030. The next largest contribution was Hfl. 195,000 from the government for consultation, training and information activities. The Ambtenarencentrum is virtually entirely financed by affiliation fees. Member organisations' fees are calculated on the basis of the numbers of their members in each of the 5 categories. Categories I to III are based upon civil service gradings, Category IV comprises members under 21, and Category V consists of retired people.

In 1979, each affiliated member organisation was required to pay :-

Hfl.   11.00   for each member in Category I

Hfl.   12.25   for each member in Category II

Hfl.   13.50   for each member in Category III

Hfl.   6.12½   for each member in Category IV

Hfl.   4.08⅓   for each member in Category V

II. AIMS AND PRIORITIES

1. Aims and Objectives

Ambtenarencentrum was originally established after the War
in an attempt to break into the 'verzuild' nature of Dutch
labour relations which were, at that time, exclusively
controlled by the Catholic, Protestant and 'General'
(i.e. secular) pillar organisations. By contrast,
Ambtenarencentrum was, and is, an 'independent' organisation whose members are 'organised on the basis of their
common profession and especially on the grounds of the
collegiality that goes with public service' (Document
GS 1979/196).

It is with this wider sense of purpose in mind that the
statutes of Ambtenarencentrum state that 'The
Ambtenarencentrum is independent of any religious
denomination or political party and respects every
religious, ethical and political conviction' (statutes,
Article 3).

The statutes further define the aim of Ambtenarencentrum
as :
        .... the protection of the material and non-material
        interests of public servants; 'non-material' being
        taken to mean the public service career-ethic
        (ambtelijke beroepsethiek).

The Ambtenarencentrum is to try to reach this goal by :-

(1) striving for "proper statutory regulations
concerning the legal position of public servants, their
families and their dependants";

(2) promoting measures to be taken by the employer, for
developing public servants' skills and abilities;

(3) adopting a policy plan that can be modified when
necessary;

(4)   continuing to make collective agreements
(<u>arbeidsovereenkomsten</u>); and

(5)   other means which may lead to the aims set out
above.
(statutes, Article 3).

Ambtenarencentrum's new statutes (dated 15th June, 1979)
have opened the possibility of 'organisations that do not
have serving public servants as members' affiliating to
Ambtenarencentrum. Hospital workers or local government
officials are, therefore, also now admissible.

2.   Policy Priorities

Apart from the aims set out in the statutes, Ambtenarencentrum's principal aim is to defend the legal position of
public servants who are members of the union. As servants
of society, they should keep up with society in income
development and other working conditions.

The following policy sectors are the most important
for the Ambtenarencentrum for foreign affairs, social
affairs, research, education and science, employment and
vocational training, energy, taxation, and banking and
credit, although this last is restricted to the 'R.P.S.'
(State Post Savings Bank). A specific interest for the
Ambtenarencentrum is representation in the Council for
Supervision of Pension Funds in order that it may take
part in investment decisions. However, it is in the
social affairs sector that Ambtenarencentrum most
frequently represents its interests.

III. CHANNELS OF INFLUENCE (National and EC Level)

The Ambtenarencentrum uses the national level a great deal
more than the European one - a level which Mr. Kenemans
sees as "still in the development phase".

1.   National Level

At the national level, the Ambtenarencentrum employs links
with ministries, parliamentary committees, individual MPs
and political parties to help it further its aims. In
addition, there is an official consultative machinery in
which the 5 trade union organisations take part. The
Ambtenarencentrum is one of these 5. Of the links
mentioned in the question, ministries are the most

important and are contacted daily. All the other channels are used only occasionally.

2. Europe Level

The Ambtenarencentrum's links with European level institutions involve either European interest groups or the EC Commission and Committees of the European Parliament, directly. Of these, the interest groups are the most important, direct links with the Commission not having yet come about. The Ambtenarencentrum is affiliated to the Conféderation Internationale des Fonctionnaires (CIF).

IV. TREATMENT OF COMMUNITY AFFAIRS

The Ambtenarencentrum has no specialised department for either international or European matters. Nor does it have any officials with responsibility for such things, although Mr. Kenemans is, himself, a member of the Bureau of the CIF, while the Ambtenarencentrum has four seats on the CIF Comité directeur.

Insofar as the European level aims of this organisation are concerned, Mr. Kenemans said that the Ambtenarencentrum puts the accent upon bringing about a situation where the best of each country's legal position for public servants would be standardised throughout the Community. In particular, he had in mind the West German pension system.

V. RELATIONS WITH EUROPEAN ORGANISATIONS

Mr. Kenemans felt that the Ambtenarencentrum membership of CIF has had no influence upon the functions of the Ambtenarencentrum, nor has it affected the latter's relationship with the government.

The Ambtenarencentrum has, on occasion, differed from decisions taken by CIF (although never on important matters). Such decisions are accepted by the Ambtenarencentrum because they have no influence on the relationship between the Ambtenarencentrum and the Netherlands government. In the event that this were to happen, the Ambtenarencentrum would resist such a decision although how is not clear.

There have been many instances when the Ambtenarencentrum has devoted itself within CIF to matters which were of no importance for national level business. One example :

CIF is an observer at the <u>International Labour Organisation</u>. This is of no interest to the Ambtenarencentrum, but it has, nevertheless, lent its support to foreign colleagues, who also want to follow a 'party independent line'.

Mr. Kenemans felt that the Ambtenarencentrum's membership of CIF had never enabled it to get a 'better' offer from the Netherlands government, although the experience gained from participating in EC level organisation had been of incidental benefit.

Note

(1) 'Other public employees' comprises hospital employees and local government officials who receive an income increase which is exactly the same as for civil servants. Thus, these employees are not central government staff, but their wages are indexed to the central government employee.

Sources

Documents : GS 1979 N° 79
GS 1979 N°164
GS 1979 N°195
GS 1979 N°196
GS 1979 N°197
GS 1979 N°198

All published by Ambtenarencentrum.

Afschrift van de akte van statuenwijziging van de te 's-Gravenhage vestigde vereniging 'HET AMBTENARENCENTRUM' verleden voor Mr. E. Boeser, Notaris ter standplaats de gemeente Velsen de 15e juli, 1979.

Interview   Mr. G. Kenemans,
Secretary of the Ambtenarencentrum

carried out by
Mr. Rob Hartman, 27th March, 1980.

11

National and Local Government
Officers Association (NALGO)

President : John Allan

Secretary General : G. A. Drain

Address : 1 Mabeldon Place,
London WC1H 9AJ.

Tel. 01 388 2366

I. ORGANISATIONAL FEATURES

1. Date of Establishment - 1905.

2. Membership Size

NALGO had a membership of 753,226 as of 31.10.1979, and
a membership of 782,343 as of November, 1980 (honorary
and retired members, inclusive).

3. Administrative Bodies

(a) The Annual Conference is NALGO's supreme policy
making and legislative body, responsible for
directing the union's general policy, and the election
of National Executive Council (NEC) officers.

Conference consists of approximately 2,000 branch
delegates, members of the NEC, two representatives
from each district council, a representative from each
sectional and professional organisation, and the
Chairman of the Conference Agenda Committee.

(b) The National Executive Council (NEC) has'complete
executive powers, provided that in the exercise of
these powers it shall do nothing inconsistent with
the rules of the general policy of the Association as
laid down from time to time by Conference'. As
Conference meets annually, the NEC is called upon to
make a great many policy decisions throughout the year.

The NEC consists of approximately 60 representatives
elected by membership as a whole on a district basis,
honorary officers and representatives of national
service conditions committees.

In general, the NEC works through standing committees:
finance, economic, publicity, education, law and
parliamentary, general purposes, special activities,
welfare, international relations, and equal
opportunities committees.

(c) The Districts, of which there are 12, are formed
by grouping branches approximately within certain
geographic areas, but there are no clearly defined
territorial boundaries. Each district council is
composed of branch representatives, the district's
honorary officers, and NEC representatives. Their

essential role is as a means of communication in both directions between branches and the NEC, and as a regional forum in the policy making process. District Councils meet only four times a year, and the major part of their business is carried out by standing committees such as a General Purpose and Finance Committee, an Education Committee, a Publicity Committee and a Welfare Fund Committee.

(d) The Branches, of which there are approximately 1,228, form the foundation of NALGO's structure. Their principal function is to advance and protect the interests of their members within the general framework of national policy and national agreement.

Each Branch has an Executive Committee that meets ten times a year, although larger Branches will appoint sub committees, and the largest will have an Executive Committee which meets about four times a year. Daily management of the Branch is then entrusted to an Executive Committee consisting, mainly, of the principal branch officers, and other committees.

The Annual General Meeting is the Branch's policy making body. Each Branch appoints representatives to the District Councils and to Conference. Branch representatives at Annual Conference establish NALGO's policies and, although salaries and conditions of service are negotiated nationally, the Branches have the ability to interpret the agreements to the best advantage of their members.

(e) Service Conditions Committees exist parallel to NALGO's policy making machinery. The national service conditions committees are not NEC committees, and although these committees, which organise at district and branch level, come under the general supervision of the district and branch organisations, they are largely autonomous.

Service conditions are almost always the Branch's principal interest, but it is a topic which will be handled quite differently from service to service and branch to branch.

District Service Conditions Committees are designed to consider service conditions problems within the District and appoint the staff side representatives to the provincial and regional Whitley councils in their areas. Each District Service Conditions Committee appoints a representative to the appropriate National Service Conditions Committee.

There are 10 National Service Conditions Committees (as of 1.1.1980) covering : local government, gas, electricity, health, transport, water, new towns, port authorities, universities, etc. and police authorities. Their role is to take the major responsibility for conducting negotiations and developing service conditions in each service. They appoint the staff sides to the various national joint councils.

Each service has a committee and the main basis of representation is nomination by each NALGO district with provision for cooption when special interests need to be accommodated. The NEC also appoints three of its own members to each committee. There are, therefore, 15 members of each and any coopted members.

Service conditions matters relating solely to one service are dealt with by group meetings on the day prior to Conference. In order to give each service group within NALGO effective control over its own affairs, since 1973, service group motions have been dealt with entirely by the group without reference or report to Conference.

4. Decision-Making Style

Simple majority decision-making is the norm in the administrative bodies of NALGO. Voting is usually by a show of hands, but there is provision for a 'card' vote at the demand of at least 50 representatives. In such a vote, representatives vote for the entire voting membership of their branch. They are allowed to split their vote if they wish, but must vote wholly or partly for, or wholly or partly against, the motion of amendment on which the card vote had been demanded.

5. Relationship with Members and Organisational Cohesion

All branches and district councils are directly represented at Conference, NALGO's supreme legislative body; and through the extensive committee structure, are in daily contact with the National Executive Council (NEC).

District councils act as a source of information and
instruction, as recruiting bodies, and as a means of
bringing NALGO members more closely together in common
pursuit of all NALGO activity, and as a training ground for
future NEC members. In addition, by far the larger part of
NALGO's negotiating on behalf of its members is done in
joint committees at branch, district and national level.

A further feature is the way in which 'service conditions'
and general policy matters are channelled through separate
machinery. This is the device through which NALGO gives
its service groups their independent control.

However, not only is there service autonomy, there is
also a considerable degree of autonomy at branch and
district level, which means that the National Executive
Council can only practise government by consent.

Moreover, 'Public Service', NALGO's journal, is circulated to all members, not just active officials, and
provides an efficient means of communication between
members at all levels.

One of the outcomes of so vast and diverse a membership
as that of NALGO is the high potential for a lack of
internal cohesion. However, on the whole, NALGO has pre-
empted much internal discontent by developing a decision-
making machinery which involves the ordinary member in the
day-to-day running of the Association. This has been
effected by granting a high degree of autonomy to the
various districts and branches regarding the manner in
which they organise themselves, and by enabling the various
services to have effective control over their own affairs,
again, by granting the service conditions committees at all
three levels a high degree of autonomy. Furthermore,
participation by a maximum of members at Conference allows
for a greater sense of involvement in the working of NALGO
to the ordinary member, and ensures a greater degree of
information exchange between the three levels than would
otherwise be possible. Similarly, NALGO's stress upon the
importance of an extensive committee structure as an
integral part of the decision-making machinery has prevented
the NEC from becoming too remote from members. Further,
although the salaried staff have become more actively
involved in NALGO's decision-making, their increasing size
has not been accompanied by the formation of a national
executive of full time officials, or members who become full
time once they are elected. The national executive members

and, indeed, all NALGO officials at branch level, and a
majority at district level, are voluntary, and this enables
them to keep in touch with their members, and to have a
first hand, up to date knowledge of the conditions in the
various services.

Inevitably, however, certain divisive issues will arise.
Two contentious issues stand out, in that they have come up
in some form or other at almost every Conference over the
past 20 years. These are the question of whether NALGO is
a trade union, or a professional association, and the non-
political nature of the Association. Neither issue has
been resolved entirely among the membership. In 1964
NALGO joined the Trade Union Congress. Hence, in the light
of NALGO's strike activity over the past two years, NALGO
has become a trade union but, because of its tradition as a
professional association, NALGO is still not as militant as
other unions would like it to be.

Similarly, despite NALGO's official status as a non-
political association, i.e. without affiliation to a
political party or a political organisation, the involvement
of government in wage negotiations, and industrial relations,
in general, renders the whole activity of NALGO 'political'
in a certain sense. Again, however, NALGO's non-militant
professional association background is still the perception
of its role taken by a large percentage of the membership.

Finally, NALGO is something more than merely a public
service union, providing as it does various special services
to its members, which serve as great attractions to
potential members. These services include : the Croyde Bay
Holiday Centre, and a vast tourist booking enterprise, NALGO
motoring associations, educational and recreational
facilities, investment and home loans, insurance, convales-
cent homes, retirement homes, a benevolent and orphan fund,
and a building society. NALGO, as possibly the richest
union in Britain, represents its members' interests in the
widest sense of the term.

6. Personnel of the Secretariat and Categories

Total - 622 full time and 11 part time (as of 1.1.1980).
There are 310 full time, and 11 part time officials at
headquarters, and 312 full time officials in district and
branch offices. The Secretariat is headed by the General
Secretary. He takes part in the National Executive Council
debates on the same standing as the members, themselves.

7. Budget Size and Contribution Criteria

Total budget for 1980 : £14,918,823.   £14,749,676 was
drawn from members' subscriptions, the remainder being
raised from miscellaneous sources, such as interest on loans
and investments, the letting of headquarters' rooms, and
loan charges to the Croyde Bay Holiday Centre.

II. AIMS AND PRIORITIES

1. Aims and Objectives

According to the constitution, the objects for which the
Association is established are to improve the conditions
and protect the interests of the Association's members,
to regulate the relations between such members and between
them and their employers, to give active support to any
member in any cause or matter affecting the rights and
interests of officers, and to promote and defend the
interests of the Association and its members to government
departments, the legislature and others.

  NALGO's objectives, on the other hand, vary from time to
time depending on the circumstances. Each field of
service will define its own objectives, e.g. 35 hour week,
increased union strength, etc.

  NALGO pursues these aims by :-

(1) collective bargaining agreement, withholding of
labour, withdrawal of labour, or other appropriate means;

(2) providing government departments, the legislature
and others with facilities for conferring with, and
ascertaining the view of, persons engaged or interested
in each and every service, and to confer or cooperate
with government departments and employing authorities;

(3) considering all bills presented to, and all
questions raised in parliament, affecting the interests
of officers;

(4) introducing such parliamentary or other measures
from time to time, which are deemed appropriate;

(5) diffusing information upon any matters affecting
any part of the membership;

(6)   establishing and supporting economic schemes for the aid of members, e.g. for financial assistance to members and their dependants in the event of sickness or death, and to encourage thrift, life assurance, and schemes of a similar nature.

(7)   providing and maintaining educational facilities;

(8)   promoting, maintaining and supporting schemes for the physical and social welfare of members;   and

(9)   making contributions to non-political bodies or public charities.

2.   Policy Priorities

It is difficult to give an accurate account of what can be considered policy priorities of NALGO and, more so, to establish the order of these priorities. The listing of the following priorities is based on the main policy interests mentioned by Mr. Kelvin Hopkins in the interview.

(a)   Economic policy, including banking and credit, and external trade;

(b)   Social affairs and industrial affairs;

(c)   Employment and vocational training, and migrant workers, in the sense that they are members of a minority racial group, but not necessarily excluding first generation persons;

(d)   Energy and transport;   and

(e)   Research, science and education, protection of the environment, aid and development and competition; agriculture, fisheries and consumer affairs also concern NALGO members, but to a lesser extent.

Of specific concern are public expenditure and pay policy.

III. CHANNELS OF INFLUENCE (National and EC Level)

NALGO's non-political status precludes any direct contact with political parties as a means through which NALGO members can represent their interests. However, NALGO has established extensive contacts with executive and legislative personnel, not to mention numerous other means of expressing its views to government.

NALGO's activities regarding Community policy have, primarily, centred on national level contacts with the TUC, government ministries and Whitehall departments. More intermittently, NALGO has contacted European and national parliament members, the Commission, and Community and national committees, through which it can directly or indirectly represent the interests of public service unions.

1. National Level

Contacts with Westminster take the form of association with individual MPs and Lords. NALGO retains consultants in both Houses of Parliament, representing the interests of at least the two major parties. At present, there are two Commons consultants, one from each of the two leading parties, and one Lord. Contacts with other MPs and Lords are also encouraged in order that they might represent the interests of their constituents who are NALGO members. Although NALGO makes no contact with the parties as such, it will react to requests from any party if it is seen to be in the interests of the NALGO membership.

Media contacts are used from time to time to voice NALGO's opinion both to the general public and governing bodies. These are, largely, in the form of letters to leading newspapers, television interviews, etc.

NALGO is also represented on the Committee for Public Services, and through other forums, in which it will often act in collaboration with other public service unions, such as NUPE (National Union of Public Employees). Representation on various TUC Committees also provides NALGO with other indirect sources of contact with the governing bodies mentioned above.

In 1978, NALGO NEC officials wrote to government ministries requesting that they inform NALGO of any Community policies that were likely to affect the membership. This request has been granted to a certain extent, particularly by the Foreign Office. Informal contacts are also in existence between NALGO officials and individual government ministers.

2. European Level

Contacts with the Commission have, so far, taken the form
of several trips to Brussels by the National Executive
Council's International Relations Committee members in
the hope of familiarising Commissioners with the existence
of NALGO and its members' interests. Greatest emphasis is
placed on the Directorates-General for Employment and
Social Affairs, and the Regional Fund. NALGO has also been
able to indirectly represent its interests in Community
Advisory Committees, in particular the European Public
Service Committee, through its membership of the TUC.
Moreover, via the TUC, NALGO has placed its General
Secretary as a member of the Economic and Social Committee.

NALGO members have visited the European Parliament in
order to identify those MEPs with local government connec-
tions in the hope that they would be sympathetic to NALGO
interests and represent them in the Parliament. Moreover,
NALGO has two consultants in the directly elected Parliament, one representing the Socialists, and the other the
Conservatives. It is hoped that regular institutionalised
contacts with MEPs will be established in the future, as
NALGO perceives that the Parliament is likely to develop
strength now its members are directly elected.

NALGO also attempts to indirectly influence Community
policy making through its affiliation to various non-
governmental organisations. These are : the Public Service
International (PSI), the International Union of Local Authorities (IULA), the Council of European Municipalities (CEM),
the European Union of Local Authority Employees (EULAE),
the Confédération Internationales des Fonctionnaires (CIF),
of which the latter is the most directly involved in
Community affairs, particularly through its (indirect)
representation in the Economic and Social Committee and, via
the TUC, the European Trade Union Confederation (ETUC).

Finally, NALGO has made various attempts to 'keep a watch'
on Community activity by organising schemes, whereby NALGO
could keep informed of day to day actions in Brussels.
These include joint representation with other public service
unions, such as NUPE; the establishment of an independent
NALGO 'man in Brussels'; joint public service employer-
employee representation, each of which has failed, because
they were not cost-effective. Various other means of
keeping an eye on the Commission, particularly, are still
being explored.

IV. TREATMENT OF COMMUNITY AFFAIRS

Promoting members' interests with respect to the European
Communities and other non-governmental organisational
activities is only one aspect of NALGO's European and
international action, which has been concentrated in three
other fields besides : fraternal links with overseas trade
union movements; investigation of trade union organisation
service conditions and allied matters in comparable foreign
countries; and action in support of trade union freedom
through the world. Hence, EC affairs are only of very
limited interest to NALGO's International Relations
Department, which was set up in 1965 with the responsibility
for developing and organising NALGO's ever growing contacts
abroad.

Little Community legislation affects NALGO members and
yet the little that does has already been of some detriment.
The 1976 Poultry Meat Inspection Directive was discovered
too late and, consequently, damaged the livelihood and
prospects of much of the meat inspector membership of NALGO.
Similarly, the Gas Meters Directive has prompted much
concern for many NALGO members, as it is expected that
"... this will cause administrative problems for the gas
industry for a period of about 30 years".

The question of British membership of the European
Communities was a particularly divisive issue among NALGO
members for some 15 years, and it has still not been
resolved. After the 1975 referendum, NALGO members rarely
had the opportunity to discuss the question of Common
Market membership until the Conference in 1981, where
reference to Community affairs was made. It only pertained
to specific Community policy proposals, which affected
certain sectors of the NALGO membership.

V. RELATIONS WITH EUROPEAN INTEREST GROUPS

NALGO is a member of the following European/international
organisations :-

- Public Service International (PSI)

- International Organisation of National and International Public Service Unions (CIF)

- International Union of Local Authorities (IULA)

- Council of European Municipalities (CEM)

- European Union of Local Authority Employees (EULAE)

Membership of CIF was one reason, among many, why NALGO's International Relations Department was expanded. Although, initially, affiliation was expected to facilitate the establishment of international contacts on a multi-lateral basis, membership of CIF has been largely disappointing in this respect. Moreover, whilst NALGO regards CIF as 'a useful form for the exchange of information and for general contacts and potentially, at least, a channel for representations to governmental and inter-governmental institutions', it does not lay much store by CIF taking a more active role particularly, vis-a-vis, the Community institutions. Hence, NALGO is more concerned to establish new, and strengthen existing, links with the EC through the channels mentioned above, than to press for changes in CIF.

The International Relations Officer could not recall any instance where the CIF took a line on a particular issue which was in conflict with the interests of NALGO or a group of NALGO members. Regarding the Poultry Meat Inspection Directive, CIF did not consider the issue, as it only had a potential effect on U.K. poultry meat inspectors. On the whole, membership of CIF has not had a substantial effect either on NALGO's internal organisation- cohesion and administrative arrangement - or on NALGO's relations with governing bodies. Greatest stress is still placed on national channels, especially, the TUC, government ministries, and Whitehall departments, to influence Community policy. Where changes have occurred that coincide with CIF membership, they are generally of the type that would have occurred anyway, due to other factors.

Sources

NALGO Publications : Constitutions and Rules - as adopted at the Annual Conference, 1952, and amended at subsequent Conferences, up to and including, 1978.
Annual Report, 1978.
The Implications of British Membership of the Common Market : Report of the National Executive Council to the Association's Annual Conference, 1968.

An Introduction to NALGO. Trade Union
Education, NALGO, TUE 2.01. NALGO
Organisation and Structure. Trade
Union Education, NALGO, TUE 3.01.
NALGO Membership B 9122.
National International Relations
Committee Meeting, 15th April 1977.
Report on visit of Exploratory
Delegation to EC Commission on 2/3
February 1977.
NALGO in Europe, December 1978.
'Public Service', Journal of the
National and Local Government
Officers Association, 1958 - 1979.
(excluding December, September and
May, 1975, issues).

Other Publications :

White Collar Union : Sixty Years of NALGO, by Alec Spoor.
Heinemann : London, 1967).

Interviews

(1.11.1979)   Mr. Hugh Bynger,
                   International Relations Officer

                   Mr. Bill Rankin,
                   Deputy General Secretary

                   Mr. Fred Magill,
                   Chairman of the NEC International
                   Relations Committee

                   Mr. Edward Alderton,
                   Chairman of the NEC

(15.1.1980)   Ms. Ann Simpson,
                   Senior Administrative Assistant in the
                   International Relations Department

                   Mr. Kelvin Hopkins

                   carried out by,
                   Ms. Jane Sargent.

12 Comparison of Public Service Unions
EMIL J. KIRCHNER AND TOM KOEBLE

The following lists in a summary fashion, and with the
help of tables, some of the major findings, facts and
characteristics found in the examination of ten national
public service unions.

A. BASIC FACTS

By looking at Table 12.1, we find that out of the ten
public service unions examined :

- only NALGO, in Britain, was established in its
  present form prior to World War I.

- The forerunners of CGFP in Luxembourg, LGPSU in
  Ireland, and the Cartel in Belgium were also
  established in those years up to 1914.

- the DBB in Germany, the LGPSU and the Cartel were
  established in their present form in the inter-war
  years (1918-39).

- the DBB and CGFP were re-established in the period
  1945-50.

- the AC in the Netherlands, DIRSTAT in Italy, FFCFP
  in France, ADEDY in Greece, and FTF in Denmark are
  all post World War II creations, having been
  established in the years between 1945 and 1959.

- the CGFP was restructured to its present form in
  1966/67.

The membership size of these public service unions
varies tremendously from the specialised DIRSTAT, which
purports to represent only 'higher' civil servants, with
11,000 members, to such all encompassing organisations as
the DBB, with over 825,000 members, or NALGO with more
than 782,000 members.

All Associations examined have indicated a rising
membership trend for the past five years.

Table 12.1

Origin, Membership Size and Trend

Organisation	Date of Establishment	Membership Size	Membership Trend
AC Netherlands	30.5.1945	105,649 (1979)	rising
ADEDY Greece	1945	110,000 (1980)	rising
Cartel Belgium	1908 postal federation 1926 present form	52,000 (1979)	rising
CGFP Luxembourg	1909/ re-established 1945 1966/67 restructured	12,700 (1979)	rising
DBB Germany	1918 re-established 1949	825,000 (1979)	rising
DIRSTAT Italy	October 1948	11,000 (1979)	rising
FFCFP France	1959	20,000 (1979)	rising
FTF Denmark	January 1952	317,500 (1980)	rising
LGPSU Ireland	As association 1900 As a union 1919	approximately 15,000 (1980)	rising
NALGO Britain	1905	782,343 (1980)	rising

Organisation and Affiliated Groups/Membership Criteria

As shown in Table 12.2, there are two types of organisations within the public service unions :-

3 represent direct membership organisations

7 constitute federations of professional and/or regional associations.

Only NALGO in Britain is a direct membership organisation, in as much as its members do not belong to certain autonomous professional or regional groupings. The regional organisations represent occupational groups and are subordinate to the central decision-making bodies.

The Cartel is a hybrid form of organisation with various occupational groups that are organised along those lines, but do not have autonomous status vis-à-vis the central decision-making bodies. Members belong directly to the Cartel.

The federated associations encompass 20 - 55 regional and occupational organisations with autonomous status, i.e. they are able to express views independently from the head organisation and negotiate on their own accord. However, views expressed by the overarching association are usually agreed upon in any case.

The criteria for membership varies between the examined associations :-

2 organisations represent white-collar workers, exclusively.

1 organisation is open to public as well as privately employed white-collar workers.

2 organisations only represent a certain section of the public employee white-collar workforce, i.e. higher civil servants or technical and managerial staff.

7 organisations are open to white-collar workers as well as blue-collar workers.

Table 12.2

Membership Criteria and Structure

Organisation	Membership Criteria	No. of Affiliated Groups
AC Netherlands	Any public employees association, white and blue collar workers	20 occupational groups
ADEDY Greece	Any state servant or employees association, white and blue collar workers	65 regional and occupational groupings
Cartel Belgium	Any state servant or employee, irrespective of region or occupational level, white and blue collar	Direct membership
CGFP Luxembourg	Any state servant or employees association, white and blue collar	Occupational groups
DBB Germany	Any public servants or employees association, whether regional or occupational, white and blue collar	46 regional and occupational groupings
DIRSTAT Italy	Restricted to 'higher' civil servants, white collar only	33 regional and occupational groups
FFCFP France	Restricted to government civil engineers and professionals, i.e. managerial staff in Categories A and B of civil service, white collar only	50 groups/occupational
FTF Denmark	Public servants, as well as privately employed white collar workers	Approximately 40 occupational groups
LGPSU Ireland	Any public servant engaged in clerical, technical or supervisory duties (presumably white and blue collar	Direct membership
NALGO Britain	Any public servant or employee, both white and blue collar representation	Direct membership

Administrative Bodies

The highest decision-making body in all organisations
examined is the General Assembly or Congress, which meets :-

every 2 - 4 years	4 organisations
every year or twice a year	4 organisations
as often as necessary	2 organisations

Next to these decision-making bodies, the ten organisations examined deploy between 2 - 8 administrative
bodies to supervise issues, policies, and day to day
running of the organisations when Assembly or Congress is
not in session, as shown in Table 12.3.

All organisations examined officially practice a simple
majority decision-making style, but in reality unanimous
decisions are preferred, especially amongst the federated
associations, to avoid internal friction and disunity.
Organisations such as the FTF in Denmark will not express
views on controversial issues if unanimity is not reached.

The simple majority rule is, however, abandoned on
proposed changes in the statutes, where a two-thirds to
three-quarters majority is required before changes can
be made.

If votes are split, the DBB in Germany deems that the
motion has been rejected, whereas in DIRSTAT in Italy, the
Chairman has the decisive vote.

Working Groups, Committees, Commissions

5 organisations employ permanent committees

5 organisations employ temporary committees only

These working groups and committees play an advisory
function, presenting material and information on specific
topics and issue areas, mostly of a controversial nature.

Only DIRSTAT deploys a tribunal that does not play an
advisory function but has decision-making powers on matters
that have not been resolved by the administrative
bodies. (See Table 12.4).

Table 12.3
Administrative Structure and Features

Organisation	Administrative Bodies	Frequency of meetings	Decision-Making style
AC Netherlands	General Assembly	2 x a year	Simple majority vote Statutes: 3/4 majority needed
	Executive Committee	1 x a month	Simple majority vote
	Day to Day Committee	2 x a month	Simple majority vote
ADEDY Greece	Congress	every 4 years	Absolute majority vote Statutes: 3/4 majority needed
	General Council	1 x a month	Simple majority vote
	Executive Council	2 x a month	Simple majority vote
	Control Committee	1 x a month	Simple majority vote
Cartel Belgium	Congress	as often as necessary	Simple majority vote
	General Council	2 x a year	Simple majority vote
	Comité Directeur	at least 1 x a month	Simple majority vote
	National Sector Commission	1 x a month, as necessary	Simple majority vote
CGFP Luxembourg	Congress	as often as necessary	Unanimity/absolute majority
	Federal Board	6 x a year	Absolute majority
	Executive Board	weekly	Simple majority vote
	Control Commission	-	Simple majority vote
	Committee Conference	-	-
	Sectoral Committee	-	-
DIRSTAT Italy	National Congress	every 4 years	Simple majority vote
	General Council	1 x a year, unless meeting of Congress	Simple majority vote
	Central Executive Council	every 2 months	Simple majority vote
	Executive Commission	1 x a month	Simple majority vote
	Secretariat	permanent	
	Regional Unions	permanent	Simple majority vote
	Provincial Unions	permanent	Simple majority vote
	Budget Committee	as required	-
	Tribunal	permanent	-
FFCFP France	General Assembly	2 x a year	Simple majority vote Statutes: 3/4 majority needed
	Federal Committee	every 2 months	Simple majority vote
	Federal Bureau	permanent	-
	Secretariat	permanent	-
FTF Denmark	Congress	every 2 years	Unanimity
	Meeting of Represen-tatives	2 x a year	Simple majority vote
	Executive Committee	1 x a month	Simple majority vote
	Sections	when necessary	
	President-Meetings	when necessary	
	Secretariat		
LGPSU Ireland	Annual Conference	1 x a year	Simple majority vote
	Executive Board	1 x a month	Simple majority vote
	Branches	1 x a month	Simple majority vote
	Secretariat	-	-
NALGO Britain	Annual Conference	1 x a year	Simple majority vote
	National Executive Council	as necessary	Simple majority vote
	Districts	4 x a year	Simple majority vote
	Service Conditions Committee	permanent	-
	Branches	as necessary	Simple majority vote
DBB Germany	National Conference	every 4 years	Simple majority
	National Executive Council	2 to 3 x a year	Simple majority
	National Council	4 x a year	Simple majority
	National Adm/Secre-cretariat	-	-

Table 12.4
Working Groups and Status

Organisation	Permanent	Temporary	Accountable to
AC Netherlands	Budget Control Committee Policy Advisory Committee (werkscommissie)	as required for certain controversial issue areas	Executive Committee
ADEDY Greece	Publication Committee Organisation Committee Disciplinary Committee		General Council General Council
Cartel Belgium	-	as required, but not many due to lack of finance	Comité Directeur
CGFP	-	as required	Federal Board
DIRSTAT Italy	Budget Committee Tribunal	as required	Central Executive Council except Tribunal
DBB Germany	-	as required	National Executive or National Executive Council but work in Secretariat
FFCFP France	-	as required	Federal Bureau
FTF Denmark	Labour Market and Manpower Policy; Working Conditions; Education, Technology and Educational Policy Committees	as required	Executive Committee
NALGO Britain	Service Conditions Committee	as required	District branch or National Executive Committee except for Service Conditions Committee which is largely autonomous and supervises almost every branch of public service working conditions
LGPSU Ireland	-	as required	Executive Board

Secretariat and Budget

5 organisations have Secretariats with more than 10
employees

5 organisations have Secretariats with less than 10
employees

NALGO is the largest, as this includes all personnel in
district offices. All other organisations only have headquarters staff, and are more decentralised. (See Table 12.5)

B. AIMS AND OBJECTIVES

According to the statutes and information supplied by the
ten public service unions examined, the general aims and
objectives of the ten organisations are very uniform.
This is, however, to be expected in a collection of similar
interest groups. There are, nevertheless, variations in
the specific issue areas which are presented under the
policy priority section. These aims and objectives can be
summarised under the three following headings :-

- aggregate the interests of their members, whether
  the organisation is a direct membership association
  or a federation

- represent and disseminate the interests of their
  members to the employer, government in terms of
  social, economic, legal or work-related issues

- improve working conditions and provide for their
  members either by representation on social matters,
  economic improvements or provide some services
  independently for the state or employer.

Specific Nationally Related Aims

Although the three categories above describe the general
aims and objectives of all ten organisations studied,
there exist some idiosyncratic features that are specifically
related to national developments in labour relations.

- AC, in the Netherlands, aims to break down the
  traditional Dutch system of labour representation via
  the Protestant, Catholic and general union system by

Table 12.5

Resources

Organisation	Personnel in Secretariat			Budget Size and Contribution Criteria		
	Permanent	Part time	Trainee	Own Currency	£	Source
AC Netherlands	6	1		NdG 1,377,598 (1979)	279,431 - (11.11.80)	Members calculated on salary, age and position
ADEDY Greece	2			2,500,000 Drachmen (1980)	85,000	Member associations pay according to membership size
Cartel Belgium	2	2		(n.a.)	(n.a.)	Members - average of individual contribution is BF 200
CGFP Luxembourg	3			LxF 3,000,000 (approx. in 1979)	42,857	Members - average is 250 Fr per annum
DBB Germany	33	1		(n.a.)	(n.a.)	Member associations pay according to membership size
DIRSTAT Italy	13	3	1	100,000,000 It. Lire	46,598 - (11.11.80)	Member associations pay according to size of membership
FFCFP France	2			(n.a.)	(n.a.)	Subscription payments
FTF Denmark	28			Dkr 7,500,000	536,864 - (11.11.80)	Dkr 28 per member in associations
LGPSU Ireland	17			Irish £ 200,000	165,289 - (11.11.80)	Membership contributions
NALGO Britain	622	11			14,918,823 - (1980)	Subscription and property and investments

mobilising a specific section of the workforce in appealing to their collegiality rather than religious or ideological affiliations.

- FTF, in Denmark, aims to develop a 'third force' in Danish labour relations specifically representing white collar workers in contrast to the predominantly blue collar workforce LO organisation, irrespective of whether these workers are privately or publically employed.

C. INTERNAL STRUCTURE, RELATIONS WITH MEMBERS AND COHESION

As has already been indicated in Table 12.2, there are basically two types of organisation - direct membership organisations and federations. The specific nature of relations with members and internal cohesion is largely determined by this structural difference and the diversity of represented interests. (See Table 12.6).

In the seven federated organisations, contacts with members are maintained through the representation of all member associations in the decision-making administrative bodies. Contacts and relations are, therefore, largely dependent on the activities of member associations. It is, therefore, important to aggregate interests at the Assembly or Congress and executive level in order to maintain cohesion.

In the three direct membership organisations, contacts are maintained through an extensive network of local and branch committees. These local organisations are represented at Congress level and elect their executive members.

All organisations publish a newspaper to inform the membership of decisions taken and the activities of the organisation. One federated organisation (the German DBB) has attempted to bring its activities closer to 'grass roots' level by establishing provisional and experimental local offices. The DBB, DIRSTAT in Italy, the CGFP in Luxembourg and NALGO in Britain also provide special social services for their members, such as insurance, travel, health and recreational facilities and schemes.

Internal Cohesion

5 organisations indicated that no problems of internal cohesion exist; only matters of secondary importance

Table 12.6

Internal Structure and Cohesion

Organisation	Internal Structure	Relations with Members	Internal Cohesion
AC Netherlands	Federation of autonomous associations	Contact with member associations is maintained through decision-making bodies of the Ambtenarencentrum. Publish a newspaper	The question of whether to adopt strike action has created internal friction
ADEDY Greece	Organised on local and occupational lines	Publishes a newspaper and maintains contact through local branches	Internal disputes are dealt with by the Disciplinary Committee
Cartel Belgium	Organised on regional as well as professional lines - sectors have some autonomy but only in accordance with Cartel regulations which are agreed upon by the General Assembly	Contact at local level through sectors which represent a wide network of communication; linguistic parity is maintained at all levels of the association	There are points of dispute between regional and professional groups such as over indemnity allowances, but these disputes are minor ones
CGFP Luxembourg	Confederation of all branches of the public sector. Sectors can speak autonomously for the professional group they represent but act in accordance with CGFP policy outlines upon by Congress	Extensive committee structure to enable all members to express their views. Publishes a newspaper. Provides pension schemes, insurance, cheap loans, tourist package deals	Main source of dispute is related to the career structure and aspirations of its members which often do not coincide with union activity and related negotiations with the employer. The association has therefore adopted unanimity decisions rather than simple majority votes when possible to achieve some sense of compromise.
DBB Germany	Federation of 46 professional and regional unions which are autonomous in their own right. Divided into 11 'Landesverbände' (basic regional unions) 15 Civil Servants Associations whose members working conditions are regulated under federal laws and 20 occupational unions whose working conditions are regulated under Landes - or state law. The latter two types of organisation also belong to the 'Landesverbände'.	Relations dependent on member associations and their activities. Publishes a newspaper and provides travel package deals, insurance, bank loans, pension schemes for its members. Has opened experimental office to inform members of activities at the local level. But generally contact to individual members is left to the individual member association.	Coordination of policies for civil servants (Beamte) on the one hand and salaried public employees/wage earners on the other, since the legal work regulations for the two groups are different
DIRSTAT Italy	Restricted to the higher civil service organised in 33 regional and occupational groups which adhere to federated policy	Publishes a newspaper	No internal frictions as representative of only very small group, therefore limited to small number of issues concerning only higher civil servants. If there are disputes they are dealt with by the Tribunal
FFCFP France	Federation of professional groups, restricted to government civil engineers and managerial staff in categories A and B	Publishes a newspaper and provides pension scheme, insurance scheme for their members	No internal frictions as issues always of technical nature and not disagreements on policy per se. Bureau of Confederation arbitrates over disputes

Organisation	Internal Structure	Relations with Members	Internal Cohesion
FTF Denmark	Federation of professional associations of privately and publically employed white collar workers. Primarily a service body and acts as spokesman for its members	Contact with member associations is maintained through decision-making bodies of FTF. Contact with individual members is left to the member associations. Unanimous decisions have to be made in order to maintain internal cohesion. If unanimity is not reached FTF will not express any views and it is up to the individual association to do so.	Tensions have arisen between the public employees and privately employed white collar workers interests. This dispute led to a breakaway of a number of private employee associations as it became clear that public employees had first priority for FTF activities in the late 70's. Also, some tension over the ideological stance of FTF which is supposedly neutral; strong leftist groups are emerging and challenging the traditionalist bourgeois stance
LGPSU Ireland	Organised along regional lines but in two divisional organisations: Local Government and Public Bodies Division and Health and Welfare which mirror the organisation	Branch structure to minimise internal friction. Publishes a newspaper.	Dispute only as a result of jockeying for better position by the diverse occupational groups
NALGO Britain	Organised on purely regional lines but encompasses a wide range of occupations since it is open to any public servant or state employee. Extensive branch and district structure but also highly centralised decision-making process	Extensive branch structure to minimise internal dissent and opposition. Publishes a newspaper and provides some services such as travel, building society and insurance schemes for its members	Dispute over whether NALGO is a professional association of a 'proper' trade union and the political affiliations that would accompany such a move towards proper trade unionism

were disputed and resolved without specific difficulties (Cartel in Belgium, DIRSTAT in Italy, FFCFP
in France, ADEDY in Greece, and DBB in Germany).

1 organisation indicated that some friction arose over
   the question whether strike action should be adopted
   as a legitimate weapon in industrial disputes in
   relation to the public service sector (AC in the
   Netherlands).

1 organisation indicated ideological tensions between
   left and right-wing forces (FTF in Denmark).

1 organisation indicated tensions between the interests
   of privately and publically employed members (FTF).

2 organisations reported tensions due to conflicting
   career interests amongst members and with union
   activities (CGFP in Luxembourg, LGPSU in Ireland, and
   DBB in Germany).

1 organisation indicated tensions over the question of
   whether to become a 'proper trade union' or remain
   a professional association (NALGO in Britain).

D. CHANNELS OF INFLUENCE ON LEGISLATION

National Level

As shown in Table 12.7, the most important channel of
influence to public service unions were contacts with the
government bureaucracy and administration. Only FTF
placed public committees as the most important channel of
influence. Numbers 2, 3 and 4 vary.

Table 12.8 shows us the frequency level of contacts with
these institutions and it would appear that frequency of
use of the channels corresponds with their importance
rankings given above, i.e. the government channels being
utilised most regularly with political parties, MPs and
parliamentary committees regarded as of medium importance.

European Level

On the whole, the European channels are not regarded as
important as the national ones, as shown in Table 12.9.

1 organisation does not use European channels at all.

Table 12.7

Rankings of National Channels

Organisation	National Interest Group	Government Bureaucracy and Administration	Parliamentary Committees	Members of Parliament	Political Parties	Public Committees
AC Netherlands	5	1	2	3	4	
ADEDY Greece		1	2	3		
Cartel Belgium		1	2	3	4	
CGFP Luxembourg		1	4	2	3	
DBB Germany		1	4	2	3	5
DIRSTAT Italy		1	4	3	2	5
FFCFP France	2	1	3		4	
FTF Denmark	3	2	4			1
LGPSU Ireland	2	1		3		
NALGO Britain	2	1	3	4	5	

(NALGO is the only association that pointed to the media as an important channel of influence).

Table 12.8

Frequency of Contacts

Channel and frequency of use	AC NL	ADEDY G	Cartel B	CGFP Lux.	DBB D	DIRSTAT I	FFCFP F	FTF DK	LGPSU IR	NALGO UK
National Interest Groups										
- daily										
- regularly		X	X	X	X			X	X	X
- occasionally	X					X	X			
Government Bureaucracy and Administration										
- daily	X					X				
- regularly		X	X	X	X		X	X	X	X
- occasionally										
Parliamentary Committees										
- daily										
- regularly		X		X						
- occasionally	X		X		X	X	X			X
Members of Parliament										
- daily					X					
- regularly		X		X						
- occasionally	X		X			X			X	X
Political Parties										
- daily										
- regularly					X					
- occasionally	X		X	X		X	X			
Public Committees										
- daily					X	X				
- regularly				X						
- occasionally	X		X							X

Table 12.9

Rankings of European Channels

Organisation	European Interest Group	Commission of the EC	Committees of the EP	MEPs	Parliamentary Grouping in the EP	Advisory Committees of the EC	ESC
AC Netherlands	1	2	3				
ADEDY Greece	1						1
Cartel Belgium	1	2		2			
CGFP Luxembourg	1	2		2			
DBB Germany	1	1		2			1
DIRSTAT Italy	1						
FFCFP France	1	3		3			2
FTF Denmark	1	3				2	3
LGPSU Ireland	1	2		2			
NALGO Britain	1	1	1	1		1	1

In general, it can be argued that European links are not used frequently, except for contacts with the respective European interest group as shown in Table 12.10.

9 organisations see their links to European interest groups as of paramount importance.

3 organisations regard links to the EC Commission and links to the Economic and Social Committee (ESC) as of equal importance.

E. POLICY PRIORITIES

Table 12.11 gives us a visual impression of the policy priorities of the ten public service sector unions examined. These correspond to some extent with the aims and objectives of the organisations.

On the whole, we can observe that the following six sectors have been almost universally accepted as the main issue areas.

- Social Affairs - better working conditions
- Economic Affairs
- Employment and Vocational Guidance
- Taxation
- Banking and Credit
- Research, Science and Education.

Compared to the national level, the European level is not regarded of great importance, therefore no ranking has been applied in Table 12.12.

F. TREATMENT OF COMMUNITY AFFAIRS

1. Level of Importance

3 organisations (ADEDY, CGFP and FTF) see EC affairs as occasionally important.

1 organisation (DBB) sees EC affairs as important in the future.

5 organisations (AC, Cartel, FFCFP, LGPSU and NALGO) see EC affairs as of little importance.

1 organisation (DIRSTAT) sees EC affairs as of no importance.

In general, it can be argued that European links are not used frequently except for contacts with the respective European interest group as shown in Table 12.10.

Table 12.10
Frequency of European Channels

Channel and frequency of use	AC NL	ADEDY G	Cartel B	CGFP Lux.	DBB D	DIRSTAT I	FFCFP F	FTF DK	LGPSU IR	NALGO UK
European Interest Group										
- daily										
- regularly	X	X	X	X	X		X	X		X
- occasionally						X			X	
Commission of the EC										
- daily										
- regularly					X					
- occasionally	X							X		X
Committee of the European Parliament										
- daily										
- regularly										
- occasionally	X									
Members of the European Parliament										
- daily										
- regularly										X
- occasionally					X					
European Parliamentary Groupings										
- daily										
- regularly										X
- occasionally										
Advisory Committees with national representatives										
- daily										
- regularly								X		
- occasionally					X					X
Economic and Social Committee										
- daily										
- regularly		X			X			X		X
- occasionally										

Table 12.11

Policy Priorities at National Level

Policy Priority	AC NL	ADEDY G	Cartel B	CGFP Lux.	DBB D	DIRSTAT I	FFCFP F	FTF DK	LGPSU IR	NALGO UK
External Affairs	1		3		4				3	
External Trade			3		4	2	3			1
Social Affairs	1	1	4	1	1	1		1	1	1
Research, Science and Education	1		3	2	3	2	1	1		3
Employment and Vocational Guidance	1		3	1	2	1	1	1	2	2
Migration Workers			1		4			3		2
Industrial Affairs			2			2				1
Protection of the Environment	1		1	1			2		2	3
Energy			1				4			2
Economic Policies	1	1	4	1	2	1	1	1	1	1
Taxation	1	2	4	1	2	1	1	2		
Banking and Credit	1		4	1	1	2		3		1
Aid and Development			4							3
Competition			4		3			2		3
Transport			4		2			2		2
Agriculture			4				3		2	4
Fisheries			4							4
Consumer Affairs			4	2	3	2	3	2	3	4

Key : 1 = very important
       2 = important   ) to the association.
       3 = occasionally important   )
       4 = less important

126

Table 12.12

Areas of Occasional Importance at EC Level

Policy Priority	AC NL	ADEDY G	Cartel B	CGFP Lux.	DBB D	DIRSTAT I	FFCFP F	FTF DK	LGPSU IR	NALGO UK
External Affairs										
External Trade										
Social Affairs	X	X	X	X	X		X	X	X	X
Research, Science and Education	X	X		X	X		X	X	X	X
Employment, Vocational Guidance	X	X	X	X	X		X	X	X	X
Migrant Workers								X		
Industrial Affairs					X					
Protection of the Environment			X	X	X					
Energy							X			
Economic Policy								X		X
Taxation	X			X	X					
Banking and Credit										
Aid and Development										
Competition					X					
Transport				X	X			X		X
Agriculture Fisheries Consumers Affairs										

127

2. Organisational Adaptation

4 organisations have a special secretary, section or department for international work, which includes the EC (CGFP, DBB, NALGO, FTF).

1 organisation has a special office in Brussels (DBB).

8 organisations deal with EC affairs as external matters.

2 organisations deal with EC affairs as internal matters (FFCFP and FTF).

G. RELATIONS TO CIF

Of the ten public service unions examined, 6 organisations are members of the International Organisation of National and International Public Service Unions (CIF); these are listed in Table 12.13.

All 6 organisations use partly the CIF for interest representation at the European level, but also entertain links with other European interest groups such as OEB, ETUC, EULAE and EUROFEDOP.

One of the 6 organisations (Cartel) lets the CIF handle almost all questions arising from the European level.

As can be seen from Table 12.13, affiliates of CIF felt that it was having little impact on their internal organisational matters. Two affiliates voiced disappointment with CIF as an organisation.

Table 12.13
CIF Importance on Internal Matters

Member Organisation of CIF	Impact on Organisational Matters of Affiliates
AC, Netherlands	small/non-existent
Cartel, Belgium	no disagreements
CGFP, Luxembourg	no effects/sees CIF as instrument for EC integration, but somewhat disappointing
DBB, Germany	no effect
FFCFP, France	no great effect
NALGO, Britain	of no importance/somewhat disappointing

Of the other four public service unions treated in this study, the Danish FTF is a member of the ETUC. NALGO (British) and the LGPSU (Irish) are indirectly affiliated to the ETUC via their national trade union confederations. ADEDY (Greek) and the LGPSU are members of the European Trade Union Public Service Committee (ETUPSC). The Italian DIRSTAT, formerly a member of CIF, has no link to any European interest group.

H. SUMMARY

What information then can be drawn from the data presented on the national/European linkage of ten public service unions ? We will look first at the six member organisations of CIF.

1. The Role of CIF

Member organisations of CIF do not have great confidence in its ability to represent their views effectively. The different membership strength and composition of CIF affiliates, as well as differences over the extent to which member organisations of CIF can (and want to) use alternative channels of interest representation at European level, are main factors which diminish CIF's effectiveness.

Two organisations (DBB and NALGO) account for nearly 90 per cent of the total size of CIF. Whereas NALGO (predominantly local government officials) and the French FFCFP (exclusively high grade civil servants) represent substantially single categories of public servants, the other member organisations of CIF consist of various categories of public employees. The strain over this and the consequent acceptance of compromises between single and multiple categories of interest representation has already resulted in the withdrawal of one member organisation, namely, DIRSTAT.

How then is CIF surviving under these circumstances ? This begs the question of what viable alternatives do CIF member organisations have ? Two alternatives could be considered : firstly, to withdraw from CIF without joining other European interest organisations but seeking direct contact instead with the Commission; secondly, to withdraw from CIF and replace it with affiliation to other European interest groups, such as the European Trade Union Public Service Committee (ETUPSC).

Because of national peculiarities, the Commission's refusal to effectively liaise with national interest groups, and the wideness in scope of most other European interest groups, neither of the two alternatives are really viable for CIF members, except NALGO.

The German DBB, the largest affiliate of CIF, is eager to withstand pressure from the DGB towards a uniform German trade union confederation (Einheitsgewerkschaft) and to maintain its special status in German labour relation/legislation. As a consequence, neither the European Trade Union Confederation (ETUC), where the DGB is a member, nor the ETUPSC, with an affiliated union of the DGB, is a viable alternative channel for the DBB. On the other hand, the DBB, through establishing an office in Brussels, is trying to seek closer contacts with the Commission.

Both the Dutch Ambtenarencentrum and the Belgian Cartel put stress on their political and religious independence and are thus keen not to have any dilution of these principles at European level via either the ETUC or the ETUPSC.

Finally, the French FFCFP, besides its stress on political independence, would find the ETUPSC as broad in public service interest representation as CIF and, therefore, no great incentive for an alternative affiliation at European level.

NALGO's national position, whilst sharing similarities with the above mentioned member organisations of CIF, also contains elements which allow for a more pragmatic approach. In contrast to most CIF member organisations, NALGO is a member of a national trade union confederation, namely the TUC, and, as such, indirectly affiliated to the ETUC. Yet, NALGO views with disappointment the TUC's limited active involvement in the ETUC and its general scepticism of the Communities as a whole. Hence, NALGO feels that, at the same time as encouraging the TUC to effectively represent NALGO members in the ETUC, it must maintain links with other European organisations and foster supplementary channels of access. This policy is further encouraged by the consideration that, with a membership of over 40 million, the ETUC is necessarily less able to represent NALGO interests than is CIF with its 1.8 million. Moreover, since the establishment in 1978/79 of the ETUPSC, and a recurrence of problems within CIF to strengthen its representation via a Secretariat in Brussels, NALGO has found the ETUPSC to be an interesting alternative proposition to CIF. The ETUPSC appears attractive to NALGO in three ways : (a) it is not broader in scope than CIF; (b) it would allow NALGO to become the largest member of the ETUPSC; and (c) it offers a well established

organisational structure (permanent Secretariat). It is
also worthwhile to point out that NALGO places considerable
emphasis on its participation in EULEA. (1)

NALGO briefly tried to relate more closely to Commission
activities by appointing a part time research officer in
the mid 70's, but has not pursued it with any rigour or
commitment, since.

In general, it has been a Commission policy not to deal
with national unions directly, but rather to encourage
them either to form European organisations or, where such
European organisations exist, to make representation via
them. (2) Whilst this policy is a drawback for alternative
interest representation, it does not preclude certain CIF
member organisations (or, in turn, their affiliated
member organisations) from being represented in EC
Advisory Committees, which deal directly with the Commission.
For example, NALGO, via the TUC, has a representative in the
Economic and Social Committee, the DBB is represented there
via one of its affiliated member organisations, and the
FFCFP is indirectly represented via its affiliation to the
French Confédération Générale des Cadres.

In addition to the national peculiarities and Commission
policy, it can also be argued that lack of EC regulations/
legislation with direct bearings on either the status or
working conditions of public servants (3) has kept policy
differences within CIF to a minimum and thus indirectly
helped to maintain the continuity of CIF. (4)

Yet, in spite of those circumstances and the potential
threat of a NALGO withdrawal, it would be wrong to create
an impression of CIF existing merely by default.

CIF member organisations are chiefly interested in mutual
exchange of information concerned with working conditions
of public servants in the various EC countries, government
expenditure in the public services and general economic
development, taxation, research, science and education, the
introduction of new technology or the training and entrance
conditions/requirements into the public service. Besides
extensive bilateral contacts in the form of visits, member
organisations see in CIF a way of institutionalising
existing bilateral contacts and promoting the exchange of
information on each other's systems of organisation,
working conditions, etc. and attempting to reach solutions
to common problems.

CIF aims at fulfilling at European and international level, the same functions as its affiliates at national level, namely, the representation of interests of public servants vis-à-vis executive and legislative institutions. In contrast, however, to the national level, it has to overcome a number of obstacles caused by national differences, on the one hand, and a complicated EC decision-making structure, on the other. The evolution of different national administrative systems and public service union structures, as well as different national economic performances and government policies, impede policy formulation for CIF. CIF's task is further complicated by the diffused EC decision-making structure in which the Commission, at least in a formal sense, has executive status as the initiator of policy, but in practice is seen as the Secretariat of the Council of Ministers and is, thus, perceived as another layer of the civil service. As a consequence of the latter, there is not the same importance attributed to the relationship between CIF and the Commission as there is between member affiliates of CIF and their respective national governments or parliaments. On the contrary, CIF and its members often see the Commission either as a competitor or, at worst, as a threat to its autonomy. This reinforces its dealings with national governments which helps to maintain the dominant role of the Council of Ministers in EC decisions. Importantly, it also means that with national public service unions turning primarily to their governments for securing interests, the role of CIF to advance European solutions and policies vis-à-vis EC institutions is undermined.

CIF's task and role has also not been helped by ongoing efforts since 1973 to establish a uniform European trade union movement, in which the founding of the European Trade Union Confederation (ETUC), the subsequent joining of member organisations of the dissolved Christian trade union organisation EO/WCL and the creation of the ETUPSC, have been major stepping stones. During this period it has lost one member and, in addition, has made NALGO rethink its membership.

Should NALGO leave, it would make the composition of CIF very lopsided with one large organisation, the German DBB, comprising 81 per cent of total membership, and five relatively small organisations. CIF could continue in such a shrunken form and might also still serve a meaningful purpose for its members. It might even pursue a more

effective role for its members both by establishing additional standing committees on relevant topics, such as
the existing one on education, and by creating sub-
committees on specialised groups, such as local authority
officials, postal, telegraph and telephone workers,
railway officials, etc. However, there is no indication
that a 'shrunken' CIF will be more able to speak for its
members and ensure their compliance on major policy issues
than is the case now.

2. Organisations not affiliated to the CIF

Of the four non-member organisations of CIF, the Italian
DIRSTAT, after withdrawing from CIF, maintains no
affiliation with any European interest groups and rarely
has any contacts with the Commission. Representing a
specialised sector of the civil service, akin to that of
the French FFCFP, it was disappointed not to find a number
of similar national counterparts for establishing a
specialised European interest group. With no EC decision
pending or planned which either affects the status or
working conditions of civil servants, DIRSTAT intends to
abstain from any affiliation to European interest groups,
or from seeking closer contacts with the Commission, for
the time being. Since it is an independent union and not
affiliated to any other Italian trade union confederation,
it has no other indirect representation at European level.

The Danish FTF, comprising a mixture of public servants
and white collar employees from private industry, and being
one of the three leading Danish trade union confederations,
decided in 1973 to become a founding member of the ETUC
and to seek representation at European level via this
channel. Two of its affiliates (the local officials of
Copenhagen, and the nurses union) are members of the ETUPSC.

The Greek ADEDY, being independent and without further
affiliation to Greek national trade union confederations,
appeared to be a 'natural' candidate for membership to the
CIF. However, it decided to join the International
Public Service Union (PSI) and thus become a member of the
ETUPSC instead. The drive towards a uniform European
trade union movement was one of the deciding factors in
this respect. (5)

Affiliation of the LGPSU to the Irish TUC was a main
factor in joining the ETUPSC.

3. Adaptation to the working of the EC

Four of the ten organisations examined (the CGFP, NALGO, DBB and FTF) have a special secretary, section or department for international affairs which includes EC matters. These include the three largest in membership of the ten.

EC affairs were seen by three organisations as occasionally important, one saw them as important for the future, five perceived them as of little importance, and one felt they were of no importance.

On the whole, the EC channels are not regarded as important as the national ones. The Commission is considered a main target of the EC institutions, followed by the Economic and Social Committee. However, most organisations registered a growing importance of the European Parliament and of the MEPs as a channel for exerting influence on EC matters.

The Wallace, Wallace and Webb contention 'that for governmental and non-governmental actors their activities in the EC are an extension of their regular activities in the domestic arena' (6) is, on the whole, not supported by the evidence gathered in this study. Eight of the ten organisations examined dealt with EC affairs as external matters, and the other two handled EC affairs as an extension of internal matters.

Apprehensions about potential transfers of government competences from the national to the EC level with a subsequent reduction of powers and authority of national civil servants and a corresponding increase in control by the Commission, as noted in the Feld study (7), were held by union representatives, but only for the long term. Similarly, whilst there was concern over increasing workload as a consequence of EC decisions, it was not yet found to be unreasonably burdensome. Generally, the unions examined were pro-EC oriented and advocated measures for further EC integration. However, the form of increased intergovernmental relations was preferred as stepping stones to attempts symbolising a federalist integrative process.

This study was mostly concerned with the linkage mechanism between national public service unions and their European counterparts and less so with the perception of

national public service unions in the implementation of EC
policies. It illustrated the problems European organisations face to be effective, the level of importance
national public service unions attribute to EC affairs,
and the extent and way in which they are prepared to
support efforts of European integration.

Notes

(1) EULEA has official consultative status with the
Council of Europe via the Council of European
Municipalities (CEM). Work within the Council of
Europe, especially within the Standing Conference of
Local and Regional Authorities in Europe, has
centered on international standards for the training
of local government staff and for basic service
regulations, as well as on local government reforms
and worker participation.

(2) Even so, the Commission does not always live up to
this policy. As Jane Sargent shows in her case study
on the Banking Directive, the dangers of deviating
from this principle would harm the Commission's role
of pursuing European solutions and policies in the
long term. By dealing directly with national interest
groups, the Commission would undermine the authority
of the European interest groups to which they belong.
Jane Sargent, 'The British Bankers' Association and
the EC', Journal of Common Market Studies, Volume XX,
no.3, March 1982, p.285.

(3) Two EC decisions have had direct implications in the
case of the British NALGO, involving the phasing-out
of poultry meat inspectors, and the Gas Meters Directive.

(4) So far, CIF has only formulated a few joint statements,
such as the one in favour of direct elections to the
European Parliament in 1979.

(5) It should be noted that the ADEDY has a member in the
Economic and Social Committee.

(6) See Helen Wallace, William Wallace and Carole Webb
(eds.), Policy Making in the European Communities,
John Wiley & Sons, 1978, p.302.

(7) Werner Feld found that a major source of concern for
the officials employed in the various ministries in
the EC member states is the transfer of government
competences from the national to the European
Community level. 'The feeling of threat to their
position was most acute among officials in the
Foreign and Social Affairs Ministries. It was of the
least concern to those in the Economic and Finance
Ministries'. Werner Feld, 'Implementation of the
European Community's Common Agricultural Policy :
expectations, fears, failures', International
Organisation, Volume 33, no.3, Summer 1979,
pp.356-357.

Appendix

European Public Service Unions

I. THE EUROPEAN ORGANISATION OF THE INTERNATIONAL FEDERATION OF EMPLOYEES IN PUBLIC SERVICE (EUROFEDOP)

EUROFEDOP was established in 1960 and its governing bodies are in sequence of priority : the Congress, the General Council, the Executive Committee, and the Daily Management Board. Its aims are the defence and promotion of the economic and social interests of European workers in the public services. The member organisations of EUROFEDOP are listed under the ETUPSC.

II. THE EUROPEAN TRADE UNION PUBLIC SERVICE COMMITTEE (ETUPSC)

The aims of the ETUPSC, as specified in its constitution, are to deal at European level with problems arising for workers in : central, regional and local governments; firms producing and distributing gas, electricity and water; health and social services; public institutions of education, cultural and recreational purposes; other entities which are controlled by governmental services; and international and European organisations, for which national governments have delegated civil servants.

Membership of the ETUPSC consists basically of the European members of the PSI and of the member organisations of EUROFEDOP. The following lists the member organisations of the ETUPSC from the EC countries :-

	Membership	PSI (European Community)	EUROFEDOP (European Community)
Belgium			
Central Chrétienne des Services Publics (CCSP)	60,000		X
Syndicat Chrétien du Personnel des Chemins de Fer, Postes, Telegraphes, Telephones, Marine, Aviation et R.T.B.	30,000		X
Centrale Générale des Services Publics (FGTB)	63,000	X	
Denmark			
Forbundet for offentligt anstatte Dansk Kommunal Arbejderforbund	80,000	X	
Handels og Kontorfunktionaerernes (LO)	40,000	X	
Københavns Kommunalforening (FTF)	9,000	X	
Dansk Sygeplejerad (FTF)	32,000	X	
France			
Fédération Démocratique des Travailleurs des PTT (CFDT)	30,000		X
Syndicat National Unifié des Douanes CFDT (SNUD)	6,000		X
Syndicat Chrétien CFDT de la Préfecture de Police 'Administration Centrale'	500		X

	Membership	PSI (European Community)	EUROFEDOP (European Community)
Fédération CFDT de la Police Nationale	1,500		X
Fédération des Personnels des Communes et OPHLM	8,000		X
Fédération des Personnels des Services Publics et des Services de Santé, F.O.	90,000	X	
Fédération Générale des Fonctionnaires, F.O.	47,500	X	
Fédération Nationale des Syndicats des Industries de l'Energie Electrique et du Gaz, F.O.	18,000	X	
Germany			
Gewerkschaft Öffentliche Dienste, Transport und Verkehr	702,000	X	
Gewerkschaft Öffentlicher Dienst (GÖD)	8,000		X
Christlich-Demokratische Postgewerkschaft (CGP)	8,000		X
Gemeinschaft Tariffähiger Verbände in DBB	60,000		X
Deutscher Postverband in DBB	50,000		X
Greece			
Anotate Dioikesis Eneson Demosion Yapallelon (ADEDY)	100,000	X	

	Membership	PSI (European Community)	EUROFEDOP (European Community)
Ireland			
Civil and Public Services Staff Association	6,000	X	
Local Government and Public Services Union	6,000	X	
Institute of Professional Civil Servants	3,000	X	
ESB Officers' Association	3,000	X	
Association of Officers of Taxes	1,000		X
Civil Service Executive Union	3,000		X
Italy			
Federazione Lavoratori Aziende Ellettriche Italiane	18,000	X	
FEDERENERGIA, Settore Gas e Acqua	500	X	
Luxembourg			
Association du Personnel de la Caisse d'Epargne de l'Etat du Grande-Duché de Luxembourg	1,000	X	
Confédération Générale du Travail du Luxembourg (Secteur Fonction Publique)	2,000	X	
Fachverband Öffentliche Betriebe (L.C.G.B.)	2,000		X

	Membership	PSI (European Community)	EUROFEDOP (European Community)
Netherlands			
Bond van Christelijke Politieambtenaren in Nederland (BCPA)	7,500		X
Katholieke Bond van Overheids Personeel (KABO)	55,000		X
Katholieke Politiebond 'St. Michael'	7,000		X
Nederlandse Christelijke Bond van Overheids Personeel (NCBO)	60,000		X
Algemeen Rooms Katholieke Ambtenarenverniging (ARKA)	35,000		X
Algemene Bond van Ambtenaren	160,000	X	
United Kingdom			
Civil and Public Services Association	192,000	X	
Civil Service Union	32,000	X	
Electrical, Electronic and Telecommunications Union - Plumbing Trades Union	20,000	X	
Fire Brigades Union	14,000	X	
General and Municipal Workers' Union	250,000	X	
Inland Revenue Staff Federation	68,000	X	
National Union of Public Employees	160,000	X	

	Membership	PSI (European Community)	EUROFEDOP (European Community)
Institution of Professional Civil Servants	93,000	X	
Transport and General Workers' Union	40,000	X	
Electrical Power Engineers' Association	25,000	X	
Association of Scientific, Technical and Managerial Staff	10,000	X	
Confederation of Health Service Employees	200,000	X	
International Civil Servants			
Syndicat des Fonctionnaires Internationaux et Européens	2,000		

Total EUROFEDOP in EC countries	448,500	
Total PSI in EC countries	2,371,000	2,819,500
Total membership of EUROFEDOP	687,000	
Total membership of PSI in Western Europe	3,827,200	4,514,200

Figures were provided by EUROFEDOP and PSI. PSI figures are for 1.1.1979.

III. THE POSTAL, TELEGRAPH AND TELEPHONE INTERNATIONAL-EUROPEAN COMMITTEE (PTTI - European Committee)

The PTTI-European Committee meets annually to review activities and study problems of particular interest. The main aim of the PTTI-European Committee is to represent the interest of PTT workers at European level.

The following lists the affiliated organisations of the PTTI-European Committee and their respective membership strength in the various EC countries:-

Country		Membership Size 1.1.1981
Belgium	Centrale Générale des Services Publics - Secteur 'Postes' (FGTB)	15,300
	Centrale Générale des Services Public - Secteur 'T.T.' (FGTB)	10,500
Denmark	Dansk Postforbund (L)	15,028
	Centralorganisationen for Telefonstanden in Danmark	4,829
	Dansk Post-og Telegrafforening (FTF)	7,216
France	Fédération Syndicaliste des Travailleurs des P.T.T. (FO)	55,000
Germany	Deutsche Postgewerkschaft (DPG)	431,000
Greece	Panhellenic Association of Female Telephone Operators of OTE	3,058
	Panhellenic Organisation of OTE Employee Staff (PSYP)	9,357
	Panhellenic Radio Operators Union	316
	The Panhellenic Society of Engineering Technologists of the Hellenic Telecommunications	1,510
	Federation des Employés des Postes Helleniques	13,236
	Panhellenic Technicians Union of OTE	8,000

Country		Membership Size 1.1.1981
Iceland	Fèlag Islanzkra Simamanna	1,229
Ireland	Post Office Workers' Union	12,000
	Irish Post Office Engineering Union	6,000
	Post Office Management Staffs' Association (POMSA)	750
Italy	Sindacato Italiano Lavoratori Postelegrafonici (SILP)	30,000
	Sindacato Italiano Lavoratori Uffici Locali Agenzie P.T. (SILULAP-CISL)	53,675
	Sindacato Italiano Lavoratori Telefonici di Stato (SILTS)	3,200
	Unione Italiana Lavoratori Postelegrafonici (UIL-Post)	10,000
	Sindacato Italiano Lavoratori Telecommunicazioni (SILTE)	10,000
	Unione Italiana Lavoratori Telecommunicazioni (UILTe)	4,500
Luxembourg	Fédération Syndicaliste des Facteurs, Comptables et Commies des P&T de Luxembourg	1,015
	Association des Agents Techniques des PTT	264
	Association des Cadres Fonctionnaires des P et T Direction des Postes	180
	Association des Expeditionnaires et Commis de l'Administration des Postes et Telecommunications	198
Netherlands	Algemene Bond van Ambtenaren (ABVA)	25,583
	Federatie ABVA-KABO	9,743

Country		Member- ship Size 1.1.1981
United Kingdom	Union of Post Office Workers (UPW)	200,000
	Post Office Engineering Union (POEU)	126,276
	Post Office Management Staffs' Association (POMSA)	18,500
	Society of Post Office Executives (SPOE)	22,567
	The Civil and Public Services Association Posts and Tele- communications Group	20,000
	Total	1,130,030

IV. THE EUROPEAN TRADE UNION COMMITTEE FOR EDUCATION (ETUCE)

The ETUCE was established on 12th and 13th October 1981.
Its purpose is to represent, within the framework of ETUC,
the voice of teachers, namely in relations with the ETUC
and the EC. Membership of the ETUCE consists basically
of the European members of the International Federation of
Free Teachers (IFFTU), the World Confederation of
Teachers (WCT) and those European members of the World
Confederation of Organisations of the Teaching Profession
(WCOTP) which belong to a trade union in membership of
the European Trade Union Confederation, or which have a
working relationship with such a centre. The following
lists the member organisations of the ETUCE from the EC
countries :-

	Membership Strength	IFFTU (European Community)	WCT (European Community)	WCOTP (European Community)
Belgium				
Centrale Générale des Services Publics, Secteur Enseignement (FGTB)		X		
Centrale Chrétienne des Services Publics (Secteurs Universités et Enseignement Artistique)			X	
Fédération des Instituteurs Chrétiens de Belgique	50,000		X	
Centrale Chrétienne du Personnel de l'Enseignement Technique	30,000		X	
Central Chrétienne des Professeurs Laics de l'Enseignement Moyen et Normal Libre			X	
Union Chrétienne des Professeurs de l'Enseignement Officiel	4,000		X	
Fédération de l'Enseignement Moyen Officiel du Degré Supérieur de Belgique	1,000 (76)			X
Fédération Générale du Personnel Enseignant	3,362 (76)			X
Denmark				
Danmarks Laererforening	46,492 (76)			X
Gymanasieskolernes Laererforening	3,400 (76)			X

France

	Membership Strength	IFFTU (European Community)	WCT (European Community)	WCOTP (European Community)
Fédération Nationale de l'Education et de la Culture, FO		X		
Fédération de l'Education Nationale		X		
Centre International des Syndicalists Libres en Exil (enseignants)		X		
Fédération de L'Enseignement Privé			X	
Syndicat Général de l'Education Nationale			X	
Syndicat National de l'Enseignement Technique	11,000 (76)			X
Syndicat National des Enseignements de Second Degré	45,500 (76)			X
Syndicat National des Instituteurs	300,000 (76)			X
Syndicat National des Personnels de Direction des Etablisements de l'Enseignement Secondaire	2,926 (76)			X
Syndicat National des Professeurs des Ecoles Normales	1,500 (76)			X

	Membership Strength	IFFTU (European Community)	WCT (European Community)	WCOTP (European Community)
Germany				
Gewerkschaft Erziehung und Wissenschaft	125,745	X		
Verband Bildung und Erziehung			X	
Deutscher Lehrerverband	120,500 (76)			X
Greece				
Federation of Primary Teachers of Greece	15,000 (76)			X
Ireland				
Irish Teachers' Union	4,100 (75)	X		
Association of Secondary Teachers	3,000 (76)			X
Irish National Teachers' Organisation	18,670 (76)			X
Italy				
Sindicato Nazionale Scuola Elementare	100,000	X		
Federazione Nazionale Insegnanti Scoule Medie	1,000 (76)			X
Sindicato Nazionale Scuola Media	8,000 (76)			X

	Membership Strength	IFFTU (European Community)	WCT (European Community)	WCOTP (European Community)
Luxembourg				
Fédération Générale des Instituteurs		X		
Association des Instituteurs reunis	1,800 (76)			X
Association des Professeurs de l'Enseignement Secondaire et Supérieur	600 (76)			X
Fédération Générale des Instituteurs Luxembourgeois	460 (76)			X
Netherlands				
Algemene Bond Onderwijzend Personeel		X		
Katholiek Onderwijzersverbond			X	
Protestants Christelijke Onderwijs-vakorganisatie			X	
Nederlands Genootschap van Leraren	14,674 (76)			X
United Kingdom				
National Union of Teachers	300,000 (78)			X
National Association of Teachers in Further and Higher Education	67,000 (79)			X
Educational Institute of Scotland	48,000 (79)			X
National Association of Schoolmasters and Union of Women Teachers	115,000 (79)			X

V. THE COMMITTEE OF TRANSPORT WORKERS' UNIONS IN THE EUROPEAN COMMUNITY (CTWUEC)

The administrative bodies of the CTWUEC are the Co-ordinating Committee, the Presidium, and the Secretariat.

Representation on the Coordinating Committee is as follows :-

Belgium	4 seats
Denmark	4 seats
France	6 seats
Germany	6 seats
Greece	2 seats
Ireland	2 seats
Italy	6 seats
Luxembourg	2 seats
Netherlands	4 seats
United Kingdom	6 seats
ITF Secretariat	3 seats
FIOST Secretariat	1 seat
	46 seats

The following lists the member organisations of the CTWUEC. Unfortunately, no data on membership strength could be ascertained :-

Belgium
C.C.O.D.
C.C.V.
C.G.S.P. Secteur Cheminots
C.G.S.P. Secteur Tramways
C.G.S.P. Aviation Civile
F.G.T.B. Aviation Civile Nord-Brabant
C.S.C.
B.T.B.

Denmark
S.I.D.
Dansk Jernbane Forbund
Dansk Lokomitivemands Forening
Hernbaneforeningen
Dansk Stymandsforening
Søfybødernes Forbund i Danmark
Somaendesnes Forbund i Danmark
Radiotelegrafistforeningen
Dansk Skibsførerforening Navigatørernes Hus
Dansk Sø-restaurations Forening
Maskinmestrenes

France	F.M.C.
	F.G.T.E./CFDT
	Fédération FO Cheminots
	Fed. Travaux Publics, Port, de la Marine
	et des Transport
	C.G.T. Cheminots
	Fédération FO des Transports
Germany	GdED
	OeTV
Greece	P.N.O.
Ireland	Irish T & GWU
	N.A.T.E.
	Seamen's Union of Ireland
Italy	SAUFI/CISL
	FILM/CISL
	FILP/CISL
	FILTAT/CISL
	UILTATEP/UIL
	FILT/CGIL
	SIUF/UIL
	UILTRASPORTI
	FIT/CISL
	UIGEA/UIL
	FILAC/CISL
Luxembourg	F.C.P.T.
	F.N.C.T.T.F.E.L.
Netherlands	Nederlands Cabineperson-Gebouw
	F.S.V.
	F.W.Z.
	Dienstendbonden FNV
	Vervoersbonden FNV
	Vervoersbond CNV
United Kingdom	T & GWU
	M.N.A.O.A.
	T.S.S.A.
	N.U.S.
	U.R.T.U.
	ASLEF
	REOU
	A.S.T.M.S.
	U.S.D.A.W.
	N.U.R.

Selective Bibliography

Bain, George Sayes, The Growth of White-Collar Unions, Oxford, Clarendon Press 1970.

Beyme, Klaus von, Challenge to Power, Trade Unions and Industrial Relations in Capitalist Countries. English translation by Eileen Martin, SAGE Publications, London and Beverley Hills, 1980.

Buksti, Jacob A and Johansen, Lars Nørby, Danske Organisationers Hvem-Hvad-Hvor. Politikens Forlag, Køvenhavn, 1977.

Bundesanzeiger G 1989 AX Herausgegeben vom Bundesminister der Justiz, Bekanntmachung der öffentlichen Liste über die Registrierung von Verbänden und deren Vertreter. Vom.21, März 1980. Jahrgang 32, Ausgegeben am Freitag, dem 30, Mai 1980, no.99a. Laufende Nr. der Beilagen: 18/80.

Burkitt, Brian, 'Excessive Trade Union Power : Existing Reality or Contemporary Myth ?'. In Industrial Relations Journal, vol.12, no.3, 1981, pp.65-71.

Clegg, Hugh Armstrong, Trade Unionism under Collective Bargaining. A Theory based on comparison of six countries. Warwick Studies in Industrial Relations. Basil Blackwell, Oxford 1976.

Cohen, Sanford, 'Does Public Employee Unionism Diminish Democracy?'. In Industrial and Labour Relations Review, vol.32, no.2, January 1979, pp.189-195.

Coldrich, A.P. and Jones, Philip, The International Directory of the Trade Union Movement, Macmillan Press, 1979.

Commission of the European Communities, Problems and prospects of collective bargaining in the EEC Member States. Collection Studies. Social Policy Series no.40, Brussels, July 1979.

Council of Europe. The Conference of Local and Regional
Authorities of Europe, Promoting democracy and balanced
development in Europe - the local and regional contribution. Strasbourg 1980.

Diamant, Alfred, 'Bureaucracy and Public Policy in
Neocorporatist Settings. Some European Lessons'. (Review
Article). In Comparative Politics, October 1981,
pp. 101-124.

Eaton, Jack, and Gill, Colin, The Trade Union Directory.
A Guide to all TUC Unions. Pluto Press Workers' Hand-
books, London 1981.

European Communities Trade Union Information, The Trade
Union Movement in the European Community. The Trade Union
Movement in Ireland. Published by the Trade Union
Division of the Directorate-General for Information.
European Communities (DG X Information) X/125/82-EN.
Brussels-Belgium.

European Communities Trade Union Information, The Trade
Union Movement in the European Community. The Trade Union
Movement in the Netherlands. Published by the Trade Union
Division of the Directorate-General for Information.
European Communities (DG X Information) X/31/82-EN.
Brussels-Belgium.

European Organisation of the International Federation of
Employees in Public Service (EUROFEDOP), Statutes adopted
by the 4th EUROFEDOP Congress. Luxembourg, 1st/2nd December
1976.

European Trade Union Confederation, Constitution. Extract
from the Report of the Meeting of the Coordinating
Committee, 15th April 1981. (81/CC-1/Min).

Feld, Werner J, 'Implementation of the European Community's
Common Agricultural Policy: expectations, fears, failures'.
In International Organisation. 33,3, Summer 1979,
pp. 335-363.

General Secretariat of the Economic and Social Committee
of the European Communities, The Economic and Social
Interest Groups of Greece. Documentation Editions, DELTA.
Brussels 1981.

Hayward, Jack, _Trade Unions and Politics in Western Europe_,
Frank Cass & Co. Ltd, Publishers, London 1980.

Industrial Democracy in Europe (IDE), International Research
Group, _Industrial Democracy in Europe_. Clarendon Press,
Oxford 1981.

International Confederation of Free Trade Unions, _Report
of the 12th World Congress. Madrid, 19-23 November 1979.
Including the Report on Activities and Financial Reports
1975-1978_. Brussels 1979.

Kay, Seymour P, and March, A (eds), _International Manual
on Collective Bargaining for Public Employees_. Prager 1973.

Keller, Berndt K, 'Public Sector Labour Relations in West
Germany'. In _Industrial Relations_, vol. 17, no.1,
February 1978, pp.18-31.

Keller, Berndt K, 'Determinants of the Wage Rate in the
Public Sector : The Case of Civil Servants in the Federal
Republic of Germany'. In _British Journal of Industrial
Relations_. November 1981, pp.345-357.

Kelly, Michael P, _White-Collar Proletariat. The Industrial
behaviour of British Servants_. Routledge & Regan Paul
Ltd, London 1980.

Kirchner, Emil J. and Schwaiger, Konrad, _The Role of
Interest Groups in the European Community_. Gower Press,
1981.

Kirchner, Emil J, _Trade unions as a pressure group in the
European Community_. Published by Saxon House, Teakfield
Ltd, Westmead, Farnborough, Hants. England 1977.

Laffan, Brigid, 'Policy Formulation and Implementation in
the European Community: The ESF as a Case Study'. Paper
prepared for ECPR Workshop 'Decision Making Processes in
European Integration', February 1982.

McCarthy, Charles, _Trade Unions in Ireland 1894-1960_.
Institute of Public Administration, Dublin. A. Polens
& Co. Ltd, Tallagth, County Dublin 1977.

McPherson, W.H, _Public Employee Relations in West Germany_.
Ann Arbor, Michigan: Institute of Labor and Industrial
Relations, University of Michigan, 1971.

Mortimer, James E. and Ellis, Valerie A, A Professional
Union : The Evolution of the Institution of Professional
Civil Servants. George Allen & Unwin. London 1980.

Nicholson, Nigel, Ursell, Gill and Lubbock, Jackie,
'Membership Participation in a White Collar Union'. In
Industrial Relations, vol.20, no.2, Spring 1981, pp.
162-178.

Paterson, William E, 'The Making of European Policy in
West Germany'. A paper delivered at the Workshop on
'European Integration'. Annual Joint Session of the
ECPR, Aarhus, Denmark, 29th March-3rd April 1982, pp.23.

Postal, Telegraph and Telephone International, Report on
Activities (1978-1980) by Stefan Wedzynski PTTI General
Secretary, 24th World Congress, 16th-23rd September 1981.

Radice, Giles, The Industrial Democrats, Trade unions in
an uncertain world. George Allen & Unwin, London 1978.

Rehmus, Charles (ed.), Public Employment Labour Relations:
An Overview of Eleven Nations. Ann Arbor Michigan :
Institute of Labour and Industrial Relations, University
of Michigan, 1975.

Rosenthal, Glenda and Puchala, Donald J, 'Decisional
Systems, Adaptiveness, and European Decision Making'.
In The Annals of the American Academy, ANNALS, AAPSS, 440
November 1978, pp.54-65.

Sargent, Jane A, 'Pressure Group Development in the EC:
The Role of the British Bankers' Association'. In
Journal of Common Market Studies. Vol.XX, no.3, March
1982, pp.269-285.

Smith, Russell L. and Hopkins, Anne H, 'Public Employee
Attitudes Towards Unions'. In Industrial and Labour
Relations Review, vol.32, no.4, July 1979, pp.484-495.

Spineux, Armand, Forces et Politiques Syndicales en
Belgique. Dissertation doctorale en Sociologie, 1981.

Statistical Office of the European Communities, Eurostat,
National Accounts ESA. Detailed Tables by Branch 1970-79.
Luxembourg : Office des publications officielles des
Communautés européennes, 1981.

Statistical Office of the European Communities, *Eurostatistics*, 7-8 1982, Luxembourg: Office des publications officielles des Communautés européennes, 1982.

Sturmthal, Adolf (ed.), *White-Collar Trade Unions*. Urbana-University of Illinois, 1966.

Taylor, Bernard, *Planning for the 1980's Corporate Planning with Government and Unions*. European Cooperation Fund, Brussels 1979.

Wallace, Helen, Wallace, William and Webb, Carole (eds.), *Policy Making in the European Communities*. John Wiley & Sons, 1978.

Windmuller, John P., 'Concentration Trends in Union Structure: An International Comparison'. In *Industrial and Labour Relations Review*, vol.35, no.1, October 1981, pp.43-57.